Geetha Malika

Geetha Malika

P. Solomon Raj

Editor B. S. Moses Kumar

Tercentenary Publication

2010

Geetha Malika – Published by the Rev. Dr. Ashish Amos of the Indian Society for Promoting Christian Knowledge (ISPCK), Post Box 1585, 1654, Madarsa Road, Kashmere Gate, Delhi-110006.

© Author, 2010

ISBN : 978-81-8465-080-8

Laser typeset by **ISPCK,** Post Box 1585, 1654, Madarsa Road, Kashmere Gate, Delhi-110006.

Tel: 23866323 / 22

e-mail– ashish@ispck.org.in • ella@ispck.org.in

website-www.ispck.org.in

Contents

Preface ix

Foreword by Dr. Sumita Roy xiii

I **Song Tradition of Telugu-Speaking Christians**
   by P. Solomon Raj   3

II **Geetha Malika: Songs of Solomon Raj**   13

Dedication   14

  1. The Destiny   16

  2. O, Son of Mary   18

  3. Prayer of the Woman of Samaria   19

  4. Praise the Lord!   20

  5. Eternal Life Flowing out of the Cross   22

  6. The Light in My Heart   24

  7. The Story of the Little Lamp   28

  8. The Love Song   29

  9. The Morning Star   30

10. My Eyes Do Glow   32

11. The Anniversary   33

12. The Resurrection Song   36

13. The Living Waters   37

14. Sing with the Conqueror   39

15. The Descent from Heaven   41

16. The Blessed Incarnation   42

17. The Pilgrim   43

18. The Creation (Psalm 90)   44

19. The Name of Jesus   46

20. A Child's Prayer   48

21. The Abode of Our Lord   49

22. The Baby Jesus   50

23. The Three Kings of the East   54

24. A Light to Lighten the Earth   56

25. The God's People   57

26. The Pillar of Sacrifice   58

27. A Child's Covenant   60

28. The Ray of Hope   62

29. The Son of Man   63

30. The Heart of Jesus   64

31. The Holy Night   68

32. The Refugee   69

33. My Sole Refuge   70

34. The Incarnation of Mercy   71

35. The Early Dawn   73

36. My Father's House   74

37. The Lord of the Children — 75

38. Who Else but Jesus? — 77

39. The Nativity — 79

40. A Light to the Gentiles — 81

41. The Song of the Angels — 83

42. I am a Deer — 84

43. The Song of the Flowers` — 86

44. The Disciples' Song — 87

III Bhakti Sahitya from the Heart of Solomon Raj — 89

IV Appendices: — 143

1. Alternative Renderings — 143

1. Song 6:   The Light in My Soul — 145

2. Song 6:   Pray, Put a Flame of Light in My Heart — 146

3. Song 39: The Brilliant Baby — 147

2. Songs from Sambalikan — 149

1. The Stormy Skies (96 96D) — 151

2. The Wondrous Jesus (77) — 152

3. I Heard the Shepherd — 153

4. The Glowing Hearts — 155

5. I Heard a Voice (10 5, 10 5) — 156

6. The Holy and Profane (77) — 158

7. The Evening (77, 77) — 159

8. Who is the Cause? (98, 98, 98) — 161

9. The Mother Earth (87, 87, 87) — 162

10. The Weaver (88, 88) — 163

11. Forgiveness to Us (88, 88)   164

A Biographical Note about the Author   165

3. Art Works (Interspersed in the Text)

1. Heavenly Melodies (Front Cover)

2. Wake Up Call   26

3. Mary and Joseph   27

4. Resurrection   34

5. Resurrection   35

6. Diakonia (Evangelism and Mercy)   52

7. Man of Sorrows   53

8. Jessie's Rod   66

9. Prophet with Yoke   67

10. Musician and the Song Bird (Back Cover)

Preface

Dr. P. Solomon Raj was born in the picturesque rural vicinity of South India on the coast of Bay of Bengal. Yet, he is rightly acclaimed 'a global Christian' not just because he has lived in different parts of the world where his vocation had taken him, but for indelibly impacting people of different parts of the globe by means of expressing his faith, art and culture. His three-fold art creations, namely, batiks, woodblocks and etchings have magnificently portrayed the Christian message through the medium of art. The non-verbal communication of the Christian message by this great communicator had been as powerful as his verbal communication through his writings and lectures in English and Telugu.

The present work is an English rendering of the reputed *Gaana Kusumaalu* (Song Flowers) of Solomon Raj. The author has now done yeomen service to the wider world, as he rendered those 44 songs of his book into English himself, and thus enables the world see and appreciate the richness of his *Bhakti Sahitya* (devotional literature). These songs not only have inspired him to express his own adoration to his God, but also have aided countless others in their worship. They were devotionally sung over the past three decades by hundreds of saints in the Telugu land of India and among the Telugus living across the globe. Now we hope these themes will touch not just the Telugus but all humans as they can now read them in English. They are not tuned though, to singing in their English rendering. These are more than just translations; with the author's unusual ease at English verse which was amply manifested in his art books with matching meditations in English, these renderings take on a new garb with originality of thought and creativity in expression. A great contribution is made to Christian Poetry in English, we may say, as the author translates these songs or hymns into beautiful free verse, and enables a wider public enjoy the rich message of these songs.

Dr. Sumita Roy, Professor of English, Osmania University, Hyderabad has done a great job on evaluating this work in a skilled manner and presenting us with a judicious and fitting Foreword. She deserves a profuse commendation for sparing her valuable time in the midst of her hectic schedule of responsibilities. The ready assistance and valuable suggestions from Prof. K. Anandan of Teulgu University, Hyderabad are highly appreciated. I am deeply indebted to Rev. Dr. Ashish Amos for bringing out this work as a 'Tercentenary Publication'. The ready help of Mrs. Ella Sonawane, as always is highly appreciated.

The essay by Dr. Solomon Raj on 'Song Tradition of Telugu-speaking Christians' is very enlightening, introducing the reader to an interesting theme. The author has presented lucidly how the song tradition had aided and inspired the devotional life of Telugu Christians over the years. The other essay at the end by Dr. B. S. Moses Kumar on 'Bhakti Sahitya from the Heart of Solomon Raj' brings out lucidly the all-time message of the Good News of Jesus Christ, presented through these songs in a simple but significant manner. The richness and ethos of this piece of literature is brought out by means of this analytical study of the theological themes embedded therein. This collection is fondly called 'Songs of Solomon Raj' as they, like the classical *Song of Songs* or the *Song of Solomon* by the ancient Hebrew Wiseman, communicate the intimate relationship between God and the devotee. We see here this Twentieth Century Solomon sharing his piece of wisdom in these songs. After all, when we come 'back to square one', the unchangeable truth of all times remains – 'The fear of the Lord is the beginning of wisdom'! And these songs, no doubt, will do well to promote such fear of the Lord!

The title covers are beautifully designed with the art works of Dr. Solomon Raj – St. Francis of Assisi with his 'Heavenly Melodies' on the front cover,; and a 'Musician and the Song Bird' on the back cover. We also find 8 other art works of the Author-Artist fittingly interspersed in the body of the text - depicting the themes of some of the lyrics. Some of these are globally recognizable and are credited with historic significance.

The Appendices give Alternative Renderings of some of the songs in this book. We also find here the author's Songs from Sambalikan, and the list of Art Works of the Author in the book. The Biographical Note at the end helps the reader know better about the background and other writings of the author. It is believed that this piece of *Bhakti Sahitya* will aid many in their spiritual exercise and devotional life. The author has done a commendable job and may this be a blessing to future generations.

B. S. Moses Kumar, Ph.D.

Religion and spirituality are the foundations on which life needs to be built if we want stability. The human consciousness has an affinity for these internal dimensions which can neither be curbed by external forces nor completely addressed by institutions. The pressures of life keep most people unaware of this, but a little time spent in contemplation puts one in touch with this deep hankering. What is needed is a concerted effort by individuals who are eager to progress on this path.

Often, what we call holistic health is dependent on the manner in which an individual forges a relationship with the divine. Religion gives the framework within which an individual explores his / her potential to actualize this inward dimension till it manifests in the form of creative expression — significant not only for the individual but for society as a whole.

In the poetry of Dr. P. Solomon Raj we find one such noteworthy effort. The touching verses which comprise this volume called *Geetha Malika* speak of his deep conviction about the subject he explores in his poetry. There is an immediacy of felt experience even when he is writing about abstruse philosophy. These profound expressions clearly explicate that Dr. Raj derives his material from experiential and verifiable data and not merely from conjecture about matters pertaining to the spiritual realm. For instance, when he writes:

In the midst of the hopeless woods
And in the life filled with absolute darkness
Where do we find a little light,
To lead our steps slowly along the way?

The way of the cross is sorrowful indeed
But only there can we find
The water of life to quench our thirst
And the life force to restore our dying souls.

It is obvious that 'woods' and 'darkness' and 'cross' are not mere words. They have behind them the power of observation and experimentation which leads to the final gratifying conclusion of 'light', 'water' and 'life'. 'Water' is used as a recurrent symbol. In a poem reminiscent of the *dohas* of Kabir, Dr. Raj writes:

Can we keep any water
In broken cisterns, my soul?
Consider it right to seek the feel of the Lord
And get the fullest joy.

Not only this, but the introduction mentions the strong stain of *bhakti*, devotion, in the poems of this volume. The *Bhakti* Tradition is a powerful spiritual movement in India, and, that Dr. Raj incorporates this into his Christian theology is a laudable attempt at trans-cultural inter-religious formulation. The postmodern age is marked by this kind of movement across boundaries without any hierarchy or privileging, and we find that Dr. Raj has made a remarkable contribution to this by his deeply moving poetry.

One feels tempted to quote many lines from the volume, but I should not stand between you and your personal response to the poetry of Dr. Raj and the message it brings to you. Each piece can be taken as a nucleus around which our faith in the divine can be fostered, nurtured and cherished.

It was a rewarding experience to read these poems and I am sure all those who come into contact with them will agree that they not only draw a map of Christian faith but also serve as a guide for the inward journey.

Dr. SUMITA ROY
Professor of English
Osmania University
Hyderabad

I

Song Tradition of Telugu-Speaking Christians

(With Special Reference to Songs of the Christian Church)

I

Song Tradition of Telugu-Speaking Christians

(With Special Reference to Songs of the Christian Church)

INTRODUCTION

We want to discuss in this essay three things, namely, Telugu language in brief, Christians in Telugu speaking area, and the Song Tradition of the Telugu Christians. Telugu is one of the languages spoken in South India and it has a long history and literary tradition. It is one of the sweet sounding languages with much vocabulary borrowed from Sanskrit and adding vowel endings to the original Sanskrit words. *Suryaha* the Sanskrit word for the sun, for example, becomes *suryudu* in Telugu with the proper case ending to the Sanskrit root, and in this example *suryudu* is nominative third person singular noun. Thus the Telugu language sounds sweet to the ear and it was Nicolous Contae who called Telugu, 'the Italian of the East'.

With the great translation of the Sanskrit epic, *Mahabharata* by Nannaya Acharya in the 11th century, Telugu poetic structure was standardized; although, free song tradition, folk song types, and work songs always existed before grammatical rules were formulated. We can understand that *Bhakti* means praising God with songs or *kirthanas*. In the Holy Bible, Jesus Christ expresses:

> "For where two or three are gathered together in My Name, There am I in the midst of them".

In Narada Samhita also we see a similar idea, when Vishnu tells Narada:

> "na ham vasami vaikunte na Yogi hrudayepi
> Mad bhaktaja yatra gayante thatra thisthami Narada"

Meaning – "I am not staying in Vaikunte nor in Muni's hearts but I am standing rooted where my devotees are pouring their hearts out in song" (See *Concise Classified Dictionary of Hinduism*, Vol.1, p. 151).

As far as the song singing is concerned, folk songs have their own *laya* (beat) and simple syllable counts (*mathra* - prosody). Much of the Song Tradition in Telugu derives its structure from the great classical music structure, called *Carnatic* music. This is a very strictly stipulated musical system built with variations and combination of the seven *swaras* (musical notes). A *Raga* which means melody is composed with these *swaras* in orderly structured system, and there are only 72 possible parent *ragas* by the combination of these seven notes in different groups. These 72 are called the *parent ragas* (*Mela Karthas*); and with further groupings of these *swaras* in different combinations, hundreds of different melodies are derived from these 72 parent melodies. All this is a strictly formalized system and derived from these classical melodies. There is also what is called light music with adaptations and changes. These songs in light music can be rendered by people by hearing, without having to learn any classical system. In Indian music, there is also the 'time beat' factor called *tala*. The *tala* system also is very much structured and defined, and each *tala* has a name. All songs composed systematically have particular *ragas* (melodies) and *talas* (the time beats).

Most of this structured method refers to classical performance type of music, generally rendered by professionals (single persons, or groups of two or three persons), and groups from the performing stage in the front with instrumental accompaniment (the *kacheri* music) rather than congregational singing. There is not so much group singing in classical Indian music except some *bhajans* inwhich one person leads and the group follows. These are generally prayer and praise *kirthans* (literally meaning praises in God's name). Different from *Kirthans* there are *krithis*, more structured and strictly correctly rendered music pieces, which are not easy for any, other than trained persons. All works of the great composers like Thyagaraja and Annamayya are called the *krithis* (literally, works or compositions).

Most of the Church songs in Telugu are composed to lighter music type, making it easier for groups to sing together by hearing and following others in the congregation or the group. However, the *ragas* or melodies of all these Church songs also are derived from well known classical melodies, making the original structures easier to sing, by forgetting some difficult nuances and without instrumental accompaniments. But the average Church person need not, and actually does not, know which *raga* they are singing.

A *Kirthan* or simple song in Telugu has a *pallavi* (refrain) followed by *charanams* (literally feet or steps). At the end of every *charanam* the refrain is repeated, and each *charanam* is related in meaning or leads to the *pallavi* or refrain. This has many advantages such as emphasizing the main theme of the song again and again, and also this repetition helps memory which is important to the oral tradition people. Many Church goers in the villages do not carry the hymn books since the words of the song are memorized through several repeated renderings by the members.

Prasa

In Telugu (not in Sanskrit) poetical and song versions, there is what is known as *prasa*. It is just an alliteration of sound in every musical phrase of the *pallavi* or *charanam*. For example,

> *Nannu diddumu -*
> *chinna prayamu -*
> *sannuthundagu - nayana nivu*
> *kannathandri vanuchu nenu -*
> *ninnu cherithi nayana*

(Meaning: Father, forgive me I am only a child. I come to Thee since You are the Father who had begotten me).

This is *pallavi* of a song in the Andhra Christian Hymnal (No. 325). At the beginning of what we call a musical phrase like *nannu diddumu,* the sound 'na' is repeating as the second syllable of the first word. The following *charanam* (foot) will also be like that, but with a different sound repetition, like :

> *Vasiga ne papa lokapu -*
> *vasudano nayana ni*
> *dasulalo nokani ga nanu*
> *jesi kavumi nayana*

(Meaning: Father, I am living in the sinful world; but accept me as one of Your servants, and save me).

The second syllable of the first word of each line above sounds the same, viz., *nannu, chinna, sannu, kanna, ninnu* in the *pallavi,* and, so also, *vasi, vasu, dasu, jesi* in the charanam have the same sounding syllables. This is in simple terms what is known as the *prasa* in Telugu poetry or song. All *kirthans* or *songs of praise* including those in the Christian Hymn Book have this alliteration, which sound musical to the ear as we have already said, and it also helps memory while singing the same song by rote.

Christianity and Music Tradition

So far we have seen features of Song system in Telugu language in general, of course with some examples from the Hymn Book. But we know that Christianity was born with a song of the angels in Bethlehem, as the good news was announced in song, which is the most important song today in all liturgies and worship services of the Church. And all through the past 2000 years, Christians worshipped in song and music. In all languages, Christians have songs of invocation, prayer and petition, confession and proclamation of the faith, and such other themes. For a long time, Telugu Christians and, in fact, Indian Christians in all languages used famous English and German Hymns such as *"Holy, Holy, Holy"*, *"Jesus, Lover of my soul"*, *"The Church's one foundation"*, and many of those well known hymns in translation. And congregations for many generations used these hymns singing them to the original Western tunes. At one time there were helpers who knew the Western music and the so called bar-notation, and also there were organs in the churches and people who could play them.

But later on Indian Christian writers started writing songs for the use of worship and witness in the local literary forms and in Indian *ragas* and *talas*. For the first time, the Church of South India in Dornakal started composing and singing the songs in Indian styles. The Church of South India in its book, *Basis of Union*, explains the need of praising the Lord in Indian ragas: "The United Church conserving all that is of spiritual value in its Indian heritage will express under Indian conditions and in Indian forms the spirit, the thought, and the life of the Church Universal" (See *Appreciating Indian Music*, p.72). Choudury Purushotham in the year 1833 composed '*Ma Yesukristuni Marugu galgenura*', which is the first Telugu Christian song in Telugu ragas'.

Mungamuri Devadas and others wrote songs in Indian *ragas* and *talas* in Telugu language. And those songs are considered pearls in Christian literature in particular, and even in secular circles in general. For a long time, people outside the Church thought that Christians do not know, and also do not care to use the indigenous literary structures and music in their worship and witness. But there are, for a long time now, writers and also performers among Christians to render their songs in classical and light musical traditions of their land. Many oral tradition Christians in the villages, both men and women, know the Hymn Book songs by heart, and they use these songs at home and in private and family worship. One problem is that some of these great Christian song writers have used high sounding bookish vocabulary and word combinations rather than the folk vocabulary; and thus sometimes, the words will have to be explained in the congregations, which job the pastors generally do. The idea is that the sheath which contains the sword should be as worthy as the sword itself, and for the great Gospel message great cultural expression is needed. Otherwise, we Christians will not be considered belonging to the culture of the land; and thus we lose touch with our own people, and fail to become the salt which keeps the society alive.

Kinds of Songs in the Hymnal

There are different kinds of songs in the Hymnal based on different genres and themes. Some of the hymns are addressed to everyone around, and these may be called proclamation hymns. There are others addressed to the one who sings himself, and these may be called songs of introspection. Some songs are addressed to God or Jesus, and these are songs of adoration and praise. In the first category there are hymns, which begin with words such as -

O, brothers come and worship Jesus
And there is no one else to save us (No. 297); Or,

To me there is no other kinsman
Like Jesus, neither on earth nor in heaven (No. 174); Or,

Jesus' name is holy
It brings us sinners to life eternal (No. 138); Or,

There is nothing sweeter
Than the name of Jesus which is very nectar (No. 136).

These are some proclamation songs.

To the next class of contemplation songs or songs of introspection belong hymns such as –

No, my soul, do not be foolish
Jesus the Holy One, the Teacher of teachers
He will lead you in the holy path (No. 473); Or,

The joyful heaven is my home
The wise one sees its beauty
In this earthy body
I reside like a pilgrim
And look at pleasure and pain as equal (No. 347); Or,

Just as I am
I come to Your feet, O Lord (No. 334).

The Present Work

The English version of the songs presented in this book are the translations of those which I have written and produced for radio broadcasting when I was in the Christian radio ministry in the 1960's and 70's. Most of them can be said to belong to semi the classical style, somewhat nearer to strict musical structures rather than to mere light and easily rendered folk music. That is because we wanted to reach the people who do not come to the Church and we wanted to bring to them the Gospel in Indian (Hindu) cultural idiom. For the same reason it so happened that most of these songs are meant more to be heard than for group singing, except one or two like the *bhajans* (No.18). Most of them are rendered by solo singers or as duets with men and women from the Government Music College, and the artists of the local All India Radio have very willingly participated in singing for recording.

Then we wanted to produce these songs for even wider audience on audio music discs by the commercial secular audio music disc companies; we wanted the cinema play back singers with popular names to help. But in those days, when we first wanted to record these songs for public hearing, many playback singers were not coming forward to give voice to our songs for disc production or even audio cassette production. They were not willing to sing Christian songs. But fortunately in 1973 one young cine play back singer kindly gave his voice to two of my songs for disc production. With his name, because he is very well known in the film fields, the songs became almost household items all over the Telugu speaking area. Later on, this great artist has also rendered more of these songs. Now the Christian radio recording studio which was started in 1964 has been closed. And there are other singers and producers recording some audio cassettes and audio discs.

The songs presented in English translation and reviewed by Dr. Moses Kumar in this book are all from the early song ministry in the 1960's and 70's. I have written all these songs and engaged professional music composers, and enlisted singers and orchestra on payment of a fee. Since these songs are fairly well known and much appreciated for their composition, message and the melody, we thought that it may be good to translate them into English, so that friends who do not speak Telugu language may also see the contents and the message of these songs. From 1960 when this Christian radio song ministry was started, for more than three decades, these songs were enjoyed by listeners. Some of these have now found a place in some Church Hymn Books, and they are sung in congregations. One was written as a theme song for the great Telugu Christians evangelistic conventions, which came once in every two years in those days. Those conventions were great events held on the river bed in our area for several days, where thousands of people were staying in temporary leaf shelters and worshipping and listening to great speakers for days. That song (No.19) is now well known as the great convention song in churches today. I, who had the privilege of writing and producing these songs, realize that my labor is well rewarded. When these songs were on the air on short wave radio, some Telugu speaking listeners from South Africa responded to these songs and wrote appreciative letters.

A Word about Christianity and Dance in Andhra Pradesh

Some of these songs, for example numbers 2 and 3, are from one of the Christian dance dramas which I had written and produced in 1973 for live performance on the stage and it included solo dances, duets, and group dances. Christian dance was not known in those days and some Church people have also strongly objected when I wrote and produced my first Bible dance drama in a strictly local cultural song and dance style, typical to Indian tradition. Fifty miles from where we live is a place called *Kuchipudi* which is famous for a particular dance form, a variation of the Sanskrit *Yaksha gana*. In the 17th century, a great guru established this dance form at that place, telling the story of Krishna, and asked a young man in every *Brahmin* family in that village to learn this dance and continue to tell the story; and that practice is continued even today. This so-called *Kuchipudi* dance form is now known in the Western countries since groups from time to time go to perform in many places.

I made a study of this form of *Yakshagana* with all its rules and structural features, and made my first Bible *Yakshagana* following the rules. My theme and the title of this dance drama was "what is the highest *dharma* or goal of life for man?" (*Kim Kartavyam*). I included the story of the separation of goats and sheep at the Last Judgment and the story of the woman of Samaria, and answered the theme-question with the answer that to love God with all our hearts and to love our neighbor as ourselves is the highest *dharma*. This dance was highly acclaimed especially by Hindus because of the medium of Indian culture in which it was presented - both on the stage as it was performed live, or on the radio as a broadcast. Two of the songs from this dance drama are included in the present collection. Both of them are songs of praise from the woman of Samaria in praise of Jesus.

Thus I tried to preach the Gospel and also celebrate in my own heart the good message through song and story. The present work is a small offering in the evening of my life's journey to the Lord who called me for His ministry. May the Lord richly bless those who read these lines!

Dr. P. Solomon Raj

M.Sc., B.D., Ph.D.

II. Geetha Malika

(Songs of Solomon Raj)

Dedication

The full moon of the Pulidindi clan –
The great guru who swam in the ocean of learning,
A friend of the young and old,
A voice to the voiceless;
A valiant leader who declared
There should be no neglected soul in the society.

> My father, Lazarus, a servant of God
> Who has now attained the heavenly realms,
> To his memory I offer these humble lines
> As a garland from a grateful son.

And long ago a woman of the land of Judea
While she lived in Moab after her husband died;
Misfortune struck her again and
She lost her two sons, O, merciless luck.
Alas! She leaving their widowed daughters-in-law
With their people,
Naomi this virtuous woman
Wanted to return to her native land;
But one of the young widows followed her
To live where she lived and to die where she would die.

Naome is also the name

Of the woman who gave birth to me;

She was named after the blessed woman in the Bible.

She in her turn became the teacher and guide to

Countless poor women in our land,

Where in is flowing the river Godavari;

She became a widow herself,

I remember her with a thankful heart.

1

The Destiny

O, our Father, God in heaven
And the blessed divine,
Lord of all creation.
The highest God covered with
The raiment of eternal glory,
Adored by Seraphim and Cherubim,
We chant Thy sacred name.

You, to become incarnate on this earth
Have never chosen to cling on to the glory,
Which You had with the Father;
And thus You cleared the way
For us to reach the realms of
The deathless worlds.

In the blessed vicinity
Of Your lotus feet,
Help us to live there nourished on the sweet nectar
Of the endless song of Your praise.

While we walk on the earth, Lord,

Where there is no solace to our souls,

Do Thou shed upon us Your shalom

Till at the end we stand with You

In the regions where there are no tears.

When the pilgrimage on this earth

Comes to its end,

Come Lord to us to stretch Your hand

And receive us to Your home, the deathless land;

This we ask You, O God incarnate.

2

O, Son of Mary

O Lord Jesus, Son of Mary,
O matchless Light!

Have mercy on us.
We bow our heads before Your ever shining
Countenance.

O, Lord God, abiding in matchless light,
Ever surrounded by the adoration
Of the heavenly hosts,
Glorious Incarnation and worshipful Lord,
Help us to see Your blessed countenance.

You are the vine and I the branch
To abide with You and always live
Bearing fruits and shine for You
Give me that grace, O merciful One.

3
Prayer of the Woman of Samaria

O Lord our God, declared to us by the Holy Scriptures,
But I did not know You nor could I discern Your ways.

I became thirsty and wandered around broken cisterns
To quench my thirst and became tired.
O, Lord, full of glory and the essence of all the
Scriptures,
Have mercy on me.

And now at last as I approach Your blessed feet,
I find rest to my bruised body,
I find now the living waters of life,
While all along I was among the broken cisterns,
Have mercy on me.

4

Praise the Lord !

Praise God, the holy and adorable,
Praise Him forever and ever !

Praise Him Who in the beginning
Through the work of His Son
Made the earth and all the creatures therein;
Also the sun the moon and the stars in heaven
And the various seasons for our good,
Praise His name!

Praise God the Holy One and adorable
Who made with great love nights and days,
The seasons of the earth,
The rain and wind,
And He Who called us His dear children,
Praise His name holy and adorable!

Once as the humankind has left His paths,
Tempted by sin and earned His curse,
He Who broke the bondage of Death

And had destroyed the thorn of Death,

Saved the earth while it was groaning in pain

And in endless misery, Praise His holy name!

Our Lord Jesus Christ, to wipe away our sin and the
curse

To make us holy and to heal the scars of our
transgression,

Became incarnate and the earth rejoiced;

Praise Him the blessed Savior,

Who died for us on the cross and rose again from the
dead.

Praise the Holy Spirit, Lord and comforter,

Who makes us wise in life and leads us along the way;

Guiding us now with none else to lead

Saying again that there is no one else to save,

Praise His holy name!

5

Eternal Life Flowing out of the Cross

In the thick darkness blinding our way,
Among the merciless boulders blocking our path,
Where is the ray to brighten our path?
Where is the song to make our hearts glow?

In the midst of the straits of the narrow valley,
Under the threatening and hazardous rock,
Where do we find waters to quench our thirst?
And save us from the dread of parching death?

In the midst of the thick thorny bushes,
And in the path of the dreadful dragon,
Where is the bloom to sooth our tired body?
And where is the healing wind to our sickened soul?

In the desert paths of the scorching sun,
And the wastes of the drying land,
Where are the soothing wasps of wind to cool our hearts
And to renew our hope?

On the road drenched all over with blood,

And in the midst of the razing storm,

Where is the possible shelter?

Wherein to hide our heads?

In the midst of the hopeless woods,

And in the life filled with absolute darkness,

Where do we find a little light,

To lead our steps slowly along the way?

The way of the cross is sorrowful indeed;

But only there can we find

The water of life to quench our thirst,

And the life force to restore our dying souls.

6
The Light in My Heart

Let the light in my heart
Glow brightly my Lord
To declare Thy path
And to people Thy word

    So that they may see Thy mercy and love
    Coming to us through the regions above.

Help me now to go
With You in full faith
And aspire to know
The wonderful truth

    Which You have revealed to our ancestors
    And kept it for us in the Scriptures.

At the advent of night
As life comes to close
Thy never-ending light
May be my repose

To keep me awake and never to fear

The thorn of death which pesters me here.

This will be my plea

To be in Thy care

Thy salvation see

Thy glory to share

To live in the place where martyrs do stay

Keep singing Thy praise through the nightless day.

The dust of Thy feet

You know is my name

Unworthy indeed

But grace I would claim

That sustained Thy saints all through along

And kept them on singing the never-ending song.

Wake Up Call

Mary and Joseph

7

The Story of the Little Lamp

In the midst of the raging winds and the rising storm
The Lord has kept me like a lamp to shine.

Receiving the oil to feed the wick
From Him Who is a never-ending source,
Abiding in the shadow of His glowing wings
To cast away the darkness of the night
The Lord has kept me to shine.

When I walk in the glow of His light
And go forward with my little hand in His,
There is no shadow ever to face
Where the Lord has kept me to shine.

Behold it is the day break and no more night,
O, traveler, wake up and take thy staff,
Go walk in the lighted path,
Go forward, and why do you tarry?

8
The Love Song

To sing the song of love,
To feed on the showers of Your mercy dew,
To touch Your blessed lotus feet in adoration,
Lord, You have shown me the way.

To quench the flames of sin and curse,
To help to cast away the dread of death,
Lord, You have died on the cross
And have shown me the way.

To give us the gift of eternal life,
And to bring peace to the whole earth,
Lord, You became incarnate
And showed us the way.

9
The Morning Star

O blessed countenance of the Morning Star,
Cast out the darkness and show us the way.
May your helping hand ever guide us
And the light of your ray always lead us.
Let the eastern horizon always be filled with your glow.
Lead us on till we draw near
The crib where Jesus our Lord does lay.

The white snowflakes shine like stars aglow
Around the lowly crib of the baby Jesus,
And the angelic hosts gather around and sing
As the baby Jesus sleeps in the manger.
O blessed countenance of the Morning Star,
Caste out the darkness and show us the way.

The King who created all the worlds
Is sleeping in the little manger as a baby;
He who rules the heavenly realms
Has come down to be born on this earth.

O blessed countenance of the Morning Star,

Caste out the darkness and show us the way.

To Him we cannot offer gold and frankincense,

Nor can we give all the pearls of the oceans as gift,

Since all the diamonds of the earthly mines are already His,

So we offer Him but our hearts and worship with joy.

O blessed countenance of the Morning Star

Cast out the darkness and show us the way.

It is not possible, Lord, to offer gifts to You

Nor to try and earn Your favor ever,

So I give my heart to You and worship, my Lord!

And become Your slave all through my life.

Therefore O, blessed countenance of the Morning Star,

Cast out our darkness and lead us to His feet.

O blessed countenance of the Morning Star,

Shower your golden light and fill the ends of the earth,

Raise the kingdoms up and lead them to the Lord,

So that they find Him and bow down at His feet.

O blessed countenance of the Morning Star,

Cast out the darkness and show us the way.

10
My Eyes Do Glow

As I draw near the mighty ocean of mercy
Of our Lord, my eyes glow with joy.

He left His heavenly home
To seek and save the sinners
To give abundant life to human race
And therefore my eyes glow with joy.

To fulfill God's great promise to us
The glorious Lord and the true Word
Came down to the earth as one like us
And therefore my eyes glow with joy.

To Jesus who is born on this earth
To the Lord who has pitied our plight
We always worship in grateful adoration
Raising our hands and singing our songs.

11
The Anniversary

We give thanks to God who kept us
And guided us along the way;
We raise a song of thankful prayer
And praise Him our guide and keeper.

We walk with Him leaving the old behind,
We cast our cares on Him to bear for us;
We know that this is a new way and a new path
And we go forward with Him with a new hope and
joy.

Falling down once we rise again by His grace
We cast upon Him every load we carry;
We know this is a new path for us with Him
And ask the Lord to keep us from temptation.

We've decided to walk with Him and never to turn
back,
We will not lay down the banner from our hand;
We run forward without ceasing
And tell others that it is a good day.

Resurrection

Resurrection

12

The Resurrection Song

He has risen from the dead

Our Lord is no more in the grave

To give us life and from death to save

Now and forever that life is ours in deed.

He brought us to the Father's realms

By his blessed Incarnation

He has broken the curse of our sin

So we all can inherit heaven.

Where else we find a blessed One like Him

Who put down His life for us humans?

None but our Lord Jesus Christ alone,

Who could our transgressions atone,

Is the victor over sin and the conqueror of death.

13

The Living Waters

Why do you seek water my soul,
In the dried up wells?
Go to the Lord Jesus in haste
And your thirst will be quenched.

Can we keep any water
In broken cisterns, my soul?
Consider it right to seek the feet of the Lord
And to get the fullest joy.

Jesus our Lord alone is the never drying spring
To quench your thirst and give the fill, my soul
And so if you go to Him with your need
He is the one who can give it in full.

Once under the burning mid day sun
As a woman has asked him for a cup of water
The Merciful One, Lord with a flood of love
Has quenched her thirst and sent her home, my soul!

Wealth and riches, and sundry power
Are not able to quench our thirst, my soul!
But only Jesus the blessed Son of God
Can shower His mercy and quench our endless thirst.

14
Sing with the Conqueror

As we sing with Jesus the victory song
We are not afraid of the mighty and dreadful
Or the chasms of death.

O wonderful story filled with glory
The story of Jesus whose strength never ceases
The mightiest song to take us along
Shining ahead on the path as we tread.

For people to cross the endless abyss
For humans to reach the glory and bliss
He laid down His life
And ended the strife.

    O wonderful story, etc.

The Lord who came as a wonderful bloom
Spreading around His great perfume
Descended into the grave and rose up again
To live forever to us death never.

    O wonderful song, etc.

The sleeping worm wakes up in turn

Breaking the prison He surely has risen

He rose again to life and has ended the strife

Therefore we sing and the ends of earth will ring.

    O wonderful song etc.

15
The Descent from Heaven

O maker and the ruler of the universe,
You deemed to live with us ?
Once on this earth,
As Your glorious grace shines on our race,
Making our paths aglow with Your rays,
You scattered the gloom from our lives.

O brilliant countenance,
Son of God and eternal Lord
Save us from Death, O living God,
We seek to be with You in eternity.

To make the withering earth
Bloom again with Your life-giving light
Shed Your rays on us again
Lord, to seek and save us.

16

The Blessed Incarnation

O merciful Lord, adorable God
Robed in righteousness and Prince of peace
Jesus our King worshipped by the Universe.

O Lord incarnate, giver of eternal life
O humble servant of God the Father
Son of God watching over the humankind
Who is there but You to show us the way?

To fill the earth with endless peace
And take us home to Your heavenly realms
O Son of God and ruler of the universe
Who is there except You, Lord?

To set to rest our woes on earth
And to give us Your matchless inheritance
O Son of God healer and restorer
Who is there except You, Lord?

17
The Pilgrim

Are you tired and broken hearted
And utterly lost walking the way?
Has the path you tread become dark
And your life weary, the journey dreary?
Just then the merciful Lord summons you to His side
And offers you the water of life
Therefore rejoice - And praise the Lord!

As the Lord meets me on the way,
What are the signs by which I know?
And see Him as He is, you ask
To know the Lord and see Him as He,
There are marks of pierced nails in His feet
And prints of thorn wounds on forehead
Look for them and see that it is He.

If I see Him and follow Him walking along
What is it that I gain at the end?
Yes the Lord of lords with mercy on you
Drives away your sorrow and your pain
And covers you with the ocean of His love
And keeps you forever.

18
The Creation (Psalm 90)

O, Lord, our King and our God,

You alone are our shelter

From generation to generation,

O, Lord, our King and our God.

> Before the hills were ever made,
>
> Before the earth was given its shape,
>
> For ages and ages, You have been our God;
>
> From generation to generation, You are our Lord.

O, God, You will beckon us to Your side

As our mortal abodes go into the clay,

A thousand years are to You like an year,

They are like an hour passing in the night.

> Before the hills were ever made,
>
> Before the earth was given its shape,
>
> For ages and ages, You have been our God;
>
> From generation to generation, You are our Lord.

Like the green grass that sprouts in glory at dawn,

The human kind flourishes by Your grace for an hour.

But soon, in the next hour

They wither away and droop to the earth.

> Before the hills were ever made,
>
> Before the earth was given its shape,
>
> For ages and ages, You have been our God;
>
> From generation to generation, You are our Lord

Lord, teach us to fear You,

And lead us with You in the paths of life.

Give us grace to serve You while we live

And receive us at the end into the realms where You live.

> Before the hills were ever made,
>
> Before the earth was given its shape,
>
> For ages and ages, You have been our God;
>
> From generation to generation, You are our Lord.

Note:

This is a typical *bhajan*. Line after line the first four lines of every stanza are repeated by a group after one person leads. At the end of the fourth line the leader and the followers all join singing the four lines of the refrain together. And the next stanza starts and goes on as before.

19
The Name of Jesus

The name of Jesus is sacred
And He is the way to everlasting life.
For the remission of the sins of humanity,
For us to see the other side of life's journey
And cross the ocean of death,
Jesus is the only way.

Jesus to make His love dwell in us
Has laid down His life as gift unparalleled
Forgiving us our dreadful sins with mercy
He stretched His hand to give us shelter.

He made the path drenched with His blood
For us to walk with Him along
And sing our songs of praise
And reach our goal at last.

He rose again from death to give us His own life
As we walked in the dark wilderness
He beckoned us with His sweet call

The matchless King to make us His heirs
Gave to us His own name.

Today our King and Keeper stands with us
As we walk our way along with Him
We sing praises all the way to Him
Till we become one with Him.

20

A Child's Prayer

With You we hold our hands, Lord
And walk along the way.

Our God, You fill our life with Your gifts
And do not caste us away Your dear ones
O Jesus who once walked this earth
As a little one like one of us.

As we take our slate and stylus to learn to write
As we walk the earth with faltering steps
Night and day as a companion
You walk with us we pray, our Lord.

As we walk with You with hearts free from sin
Following Your footprints true and faithful
We walk with righteousness, Our Lord
And remain Your true children in deed.

21
The Abode of Our Lord

My heart is lighted up with His light
My mind blooms like a flower
My foot becomes quick
As I approach the abode of my Lord.

The sweet songs and the loving calls
And the shining pearls of the whitest snow
As I hear with my ears and see with my eyes
My heart became filled with His light.

As the descent of the heavenly hosts
And the coming down of the glorious light
To make the earth rejoice in mirth
My heart becomes filled with His light.

To the poor realms of the unrighteous destitutes
The King Himself stooped down to earth
And became a babe in Bethlehem's inn
As I hear this wonderful story heart rejoices.

22
The Baby Jesus

The ruler of the heavenly realms
Is born today to save us.
And we believe it is true
That He will never again leave us.

In the face of the little babe
Bright light shines forth
And scatters away the darkness
To the tired worlds as it gives peace.

The ruler of the heavenly realms
Is born today to save us.

In the golden curls of the little babe
The tinkling stars shine
To lead us on the path not straying
And take us safely home.

A heavenly light glows on His face
That is the source of life for heaven and earth
To give solace to our tired souls
And make us sing along the way.

The golden circle surrounding His head

Is the great and glorious crown

To tell us that He is the King of kings

He the ruler of the universe is born today.

Diakonia (Evangelism and Mercy)

Man of Sorrows

23
The Three Kings
of the East

They came to pay homage to the King of kings
The wise men of the East, the kings of this earth;
To kneel down and worship Him
To sing praises and declare Him as the heavenly King
They came to pay homage the kings of the East.

So that we may also seek You and find
To see with our eyes the ocean of mercy
The wise men of the East seeing the star
They traveled far remembering the Scriptures
They came to pay homage to the King of kings.

So that our feet may find the way
And to follow Your path without mistake
We too come to Thy lowly manger
And kneel down like them to pay our homage
They came to pay homage the kings of the East.

For us to bring to You our body and mind

To offer them to You at Your holy lotus feet

With these our gifts to make devotion

And to ask in return Your endless blessing,

They came to pay homage to the King of kings.

24

A Light to Lighten the Earth

As the brightest light shines in the sky
The gloom of the earth was cast away.

The thickest night and the blindening darkness
Melted down as the ray shined in people's eye
And their countenance went aglow.

The broken hearts of the oppressed race
Got redeemed from nagging doubt and great despair
As the newest song of the Savior's love
Comes and fills the earth today
The fear of death has been driven away.

25

The God's People

O, people of Israel, turn today to God
And seek the shelter under the arm
Of the Lord Who will never forget
His promises made to you.

O, people of God, know the ways of His truth
And seek the strength of the Lord
Come again to the Savior
And ask for His blessing for you.

If humans seek Him His favor to show
And return to ask His mercy now
He is ready to take pity again
And show you again His salvation.

Ye all the nations of the earth again
Gather around His mighty throne
Pay your homage and at His feet do fall
And worship Jesus Lord of all.

26

The Pillar of Sacrifice

Where did Jesus die on the cross?
And where did He make the sacrifice?

In the world where humanity was cursed with sin
And where it was thrown in the abyss of death
There dear Jesus before our eyes
Laid His life and died on the cross.
 Where did Jesus die on the cross?

Outside the city walls and by the wayside sun
In the scorching day light in the terrible noon
In agony which no one had ever did suffer
He died for us and yet He lives forever.
 Where did Jesus die on the cross?

For us the sinning and helpless souls
He came down even from the heavenly realms
Through His death to give us heavenly bliss
And bring to us God's forgiveness.
 Where did Jesus die on the cross?

To the helpless creatures seeking in vain

The living waters in dried up wells

He came to bring us to God again

And to bliss with which He always fills.

Where did Jesus die on the cross?

When the human race went astray and missed the path

And became blind and merited God's wrath

Jesus our Lord brought His great salvation

And between God and man a great reconciliation.

Where did Jesus die on the cross?

27

A Child's Covenant

We little children soldiers of Christ
We walk ahead holding His cross in our hands
To conquer the evils of the earth
And to win the war against Satan.

We hear the call of the Lord
And walk faithfully with Him
To go along the righteous path
And never ever to go astray.

We are the sheep of our Lord
We shall never be in want
We along the shores of living water
Both day and night in His keeping.

We are the playmates of Baby Jesus
We learn from Him mercy and love
So that we seek and serve all our neighbors
In His name without ceasing.

We wear the armor of righteousness
And walk with Him in the holy path
Holding fast in our hands
The swiftest sword of His holy word.

We are warriors of the white robes
We will never fear any foes
And we shall abide in the blessed arms
Of Him Who has conquered death.

28

The Ray of Hope

O ray of hope of our ancient fathers
Lead us through the deathless path
So that we may keep looking at You
And attain the land of peace at the end.

Here on the earth in hunger and pain
Fear of death and never ending strain
They will never darken our view
Till we cross the ocean of life and rise in victory.

Once our fathers walked in paths of tribulation
They never lost hope in their hearts
But with great courage and faith
They walked ahead and reached their goal.

O ray of hope You're the power of God
You lead all people in Your fearless path
Till the rulers of this earth bow down before You
And all creatures live under the rule of love.

29

The Son of Man

O Son of Man, brilliant glory
Merciful Lord, conqueror of death
The way of life and Savior divine
Show Your mercy and save us, Lord!

For us humans You came to the earth
You died on the cross and rose again
By the blood which flowed from Your side
You cleanse us from our sins, O Lord!

In the burden of sin and curse and death
The world of ours has drowned in abyss
O Lord of love and treasure to the earth
You opened the gates of eternal life!

30
The Heart of Jesus

Has this world ever known the heart of Jesus Christ?
Has the human race ever & ought the meaning of the Scriptures?

When masses held the palm branches high
And when they cried out loudly saying victories to Jesus
Has the world really known the heart of Jesus?
And has the human race ever sought to known the Scriptures?

When once two brothers sought great positions
And so sought places on the right and left of Christ
Have the people of the earth known the heart of Jesus?
Has the world ever understood the meaning of the Scriptures?

When Jesus Himself stoopped down to wash the feet of his disciples
And when they looked at Him with dismay and fear
Has the world tried to know the heart of Jesus?
And did the world known the meaning of the Scriptures?

When the Lord fed five thousand people

In the midst of the desert with five loaves and two fish

Have the people known who Jesus really was?

And has the world known the meaning of the
Scriptures?

When the Son of Man said that He had to die on the
cross

And lay down His life for the remission of our sins

Did people understand what He was saying?

Did the world know this is the fulfillment of the
Scripture?

When Christ rose again from the grave and stood

In the midst of the disciples, did they know that it was
true?

Some people cannot see even if they have eyes to see!

And some people cannot hear even if they have ears to
hear!

Jessie's Rod

Prophet with Yoke

31
The Holy Night

The four corners of the earth calmly slept
And thick darkness had covered like blanket the earth
Silence ruled the whole creation
When God Himself became a man and was born on
the earth.

A great star showed its countenance in the sky
Hosts of angels came down to earth
To sing praises and wake up men
When our Lord Jesus came as a baby.

Mary of Bethlehem did not forget the angelic vision
The mystery still lingered in her mind
The Holy Spirit still ruled in her heart
When the baby Jesus slept in the manger.

But the darkness of sin has fled in flight
The curse on mankind rolled away then
The presence of God to be with the earth
When God Himself came down to the earth.

32
The Refugee

Who else but You
To save me and keep me, Lord?
No one but You is the gift-giver of life,
And the beloved of my heart
I shall never forget You.

When I sought Your love
And came to You in faith
You without hiding Your face to me
Have beckoned me to Your bosom.

Even if my mother and father reject me
From You I get all I need
And You comfort me more than
My mother and father can do.

I desire to abide with You
Both here and hereafter
I ask You to subdue my 'self'
And keep me ever in You.

33

My Sole Refuge

O, Jesus the giver of life!
Only in You is my refuge;
I ask You to keep me safe
Both night and day always.

Since You have shown pity
And You will never
Leave me desolate,
And I worship you.

Your body of marvelous glory,
You have given to us for sustenance;
And the divine nectar is Your blood,
You gave so we receive to become deathless.

Standing steadfast in the realms of faith,
We worship You today without ceasing;
And conquer sickness and death,
And step forward with You in eternal joy.

On the day when the eternal city
Becomes our everlasting abode,
When we rejoice in the never ending glory,
We shall have the bliss of Your countenance.

34

The Incarnation of Mercy

Have mercy on me, O loving One!
Have mercy on me since I come to Thee,
Seeking Your mercy!

> Because I am a sinner I'm filled with fear,
> I lost all peace in my heart.
> Seeking Your mercy I am coming to You,
> Have mercy on me, O Lord!

For too long I was desiring
Your matchless treasure of kindness
And now I come to You!

> Cast out my fear of mortal body;
> Draw me to Your safe bosom,
> Give me full victory which is with You;
> Have mercy on me, O Lord!

Give me the whitest robe
And fill my ears with Your
Sweetest beckoning call.

Make the realms of my heart
Filled with an abiding peace
And keep Your thoughts always in me
Have mercy on me, O Lord!
Break the rock of my heart!
So that tears of regret freely flow
And wash away my sins.

Give me a renewed heart
And the raiment of righteousness
Holding me by our hand,
Lord, lead me on!

35
The Early Dawn

The golden rays awaken me

All the corners of the earth are waking up

At this breaking of the day

I stand at Your door seeking to know Your will.

A sweet flavor to life and the best of gifts

A way to help others who are in need

That is what today is for me, You tell me

And You showed me the way to life.

Yesterday has melted away like a night's dream

Tomorrow is something I cannot foresee

Only today is the wealth in my hand

A precious diamond the tide of time brings to me.

36

My Father's House

Verily the Lord is my light and salvation
I shall not be afraid of anyone in the world;
Verily the Lord is my strong fortress
I shall not fear any danger.

If all races rise up to kill me
Even if all my enemies rise up to destroy
And an army comes down to fight with me
I shall not be afraid nor shall I fear.

To stay in the Lord's house,
To hide in the bosom of the Father
To abide with Him without fear
This I consider as the endless Fortune.

I shall abide in the courts of my Lord
I shall forget myself playing and singing there
Giving thanks to Him and sing His praises again
And sing His songs in a thousand tongues.

37

The Lord of the Children

Who is the companion to us little ones?
And who is our everlasting friend?
Who is the commander of us little soldiers?
And who is the ruler?

Who is the leader on the earth leading us?
And who is the wayfarer walking with us here?
And who is the master showering His blessings?
And who shows us the path of righteousness?

The Kingdom of God is of the little ones
Let them come to Me, He said.
Who is that blessed Lord who laid His hands
To bless us, and hugged us with love?

Coming as the dear Son of the virgin Mary
Treading this earth like one of us little ones
The glorious Lord the creator of this earth
Who is that Lord of life who conquered death?

Who is the loving host who gives us
The robes of righteousness and everlasting life?
When we finish life's journey at the end
and reach our home,
Who is the Lord who takes us into His home?

38

Who Else but Jesus?

Who is the merciful Lord,
To quench my thirst
And give me solace?
And who is the merciful Lord
Who even now rules in my life?

Who is the God who makes me stand
In the heavenly realms -
Where there is the endless joy?
Who is the One who leads me on day by day,
Who else but Jesus my Lord?

Wiping away the agonizing fear of guilt,
Bringing down the loads from my shoulders,
Who gives shelter to my helpless head?
Who is it who calls me to His bosom when I am tired?
Who else but Jesus my Lord?

To keep me company in my earthly journey
Not for a moment leaving me alone,

To put His merciful hand on my bruised head,
To carry all my woes and wipe away my tears,
Who else is there but the Lord Jesus?

Who is it who comes to hold my hand
As I breathe here my last?
Who is He that takes me home with Him?
Who else but Jesus my Lord - who died in my place,
And rose again to live forever?

39
The Nativity

As the illumination of the golden stars
Came to lighten the earth's corners
Was born in the manger the Savior, our Lord
The incarnation of the Logos and the Son of God.

People who kept waiting for Him today rejoice
And celebrate the year of Jubilee and hear God's voice
Indeed He came to the earth as God's greatest gift
To reconcile God to man and stop the rift.

To redeem the humanity from death He came
Son of God and Son of Man and Savior is His name
Of the womb of Mary the blessed Mother, thrice virgin
Immanuel, that is God with us, humble, loving and lowly.

People of this earth with His might to win the deadly fight
And reach the heavenly realms where there is no never night

He made a promise long ago and fulfilled it today

And by His advent to the earth He has driven our fears away.

The darkness of ignorance has fled in His mighty light

The heavenly Guru by His light has put our fear to flight

And He beckoned us to join and walk with the heavenly hosts

Till at the end we ever live with the Father, Him and the Holy Ghost.

40

A Light to the Gentiles

As the mercy of the Lord
Shone on the nations
The earth became lighted up
Death itself became mortal.
    Curse moved away
    As God became man in the womb of Mary.

Christ the Son God
From heaven He descended
To save the earth from peril
And to redeem the Adam's race.
    With immeasurable mercy
    He came to abide with us.

Jesus the sun of the world
Had caste His kindly looks
On us miserable sinners
And made our lives bright.

For us to walk on the deathless path
He gave His likeness to the mortals.

The mortals of this earth
Shall live in grace and peace
By this the gift of His son
And shall at the end will inherit heaven.
So glory to God and goodwill to men
And well being to people who are humble.
To redeem from our burdens
The Lord Himself has come down.
Like one of us in a woman's womb
He came to the earth and lived with us.

Those who came to Him with hunger
He filled them with good gifts
But those who came with pride and plenty
He sent them out empty handed.

41

The Song of the Angels

Glory to God in the highest,
And peace and well being
To God's blessed ones on the earth.

The Son of God came to the earth
To bear our heavy loads.
He became human born to virgin.
    Glory to God in the highest...

The very Son of God drove out the darkness
So the world may not be caught
In the terrible darkness of sin.
    Glory to God in the highest...

He fed those who came to him hungry
And sent away the proud with empty hands.
    Glory to God in the highest...

42
I am a Deer

Like the deer thirsty for cool waters
So my heart gets thirsty for the love of my Lord.

In the fellowship of that Lord
There is a feast to my heart
Such a fellowship to share
I will not find anywhere.
So when my throat turns dry
I to the Lord's bosom fly
By the shores of the clearest waters
My Lord in grace appears.

When He once comes near
There is no shadow of fear
Since He takes me to His side
And from danger surely will hide.
When I run away from the foes
I shall tell Him all my woes
And the Lord of the lotus feet
Will all my needs then meet.

All my doubts and fears
I shall now put in His ears
My Lord of golden main
Shall never send me in vain.
Where else shall I get the peace?
And where else my rest increase?
Except with You my Lord
There is no real concord.

43
The Song of the Flowers

We are little tender flower plants
We are lovely singing parrots
We sway about in the wind
And sing and play around.

We bloom with lovely flowers
We scatter around the moonlight
We send out sweet odors
And call the honey bee as friend.

We join each other our hands
To say that we are truly friends
We seek for a daily growing
And pray for the Lord's blessing.

The Disciples' Song

Lord our hearts are lighted
As we, Your great countenance behold.

Can we ever forget You, our beloved?
And can we depart from Your blessed feet?
We do not want to go where You're not
With You we have all that we want.

Have mercy blessed Lord,
And receive us poor creatures.

Come and save, blessed Jesus!
You are the only One who pitied us and saved.
O, giver of life and merciful Lord,
Open the doors of heavenly gates,
Send into our hearts Your breath to abide.

Have mercy, O Lord and leave us not,
And we steadfastly will cling on to Thee.

III. Bhakti Sahitya from the Heart

of Solomon Raj

III.

Bhakti Sahitya from the Heart of Solomon Raj

INTRODUCTION

The devotion or feeling of oneness of humans which recognizes the greatness of God and endeavors to express it in terms of praise and adoration is what we may call *'Bhakti'*. The word, *Bhakti* is derived from the Sanskrit root *bhaj* which means 'to revere'. It connotes respectful devotion marked by 'intense personal attachment to God' which springs, for a Christian, from an unshakable trust in an awesome and adorable God. There is the dynamics of *'Saameepya'* (nearness or intimacy) between God and the devotee–building bridges and ensuing 'I-Thou' relationship. In Bhagavad Gita, the word *bhakti* is used in combination of another word, *prapathi* – which means utter dependence on God. The two popular streams through which the *Bhatki* of a people in general or of a person in particular flows are the *Sahitya* (literature), and *Sangeetha* (song or music). A culmination may be seen in a combination of both – the verse in tune!

The present study pertains to such an exercise in one of the writings of Dr. P. Solomon Raj, entitled *'Gaana Kusumaalu'* (Song Flowers), which is one of the outstanding examples of

Bhakti Sahitya in Telugu. In his preface to this book in Telugu, Karanam Balasubrahmanyam Pille aptly remarked that though Dr. Solomon Raj might have written countless books before, his life attained its fulfillment just with these lyrics.[1] Dr. Job Sudarshan feels that the author being a unique artist had presented these songs as beautiful 'word pictures'.[2] A brief survey of the writings of Solomon Raj in Telugu will be presented in the following pages before we plunge into the depths of the main work under present study.

SOME MAJOR WORKS OF DR. RAJ IN TELUGU

The most significant writings of Solomon Raj in Telugu are a handful of his varied attempts to bring out his reflections on different religious themes through different literary forms. *Puja Mandiram* (Temple of Worship), his earlier literary creation in Telugu, was a *dwipada kaavya* (verse in couplets). It is rather a poetic expression of 'I-Thou' relationship between a devotee and his God, and the author exhibits therein his heart as a 'temple of worship'. The refrain is :

> Lord, I make my heart a temple
>
> To offer my worship to You!

His next writing in Telugu, *Eeshodaharanam* is an illustrative poetic exercise in portraying Jesus. It is a captivating call to Jesus in all the case-endings of Christ's name - each in one verse. This work follows the great tradition of some great Hindu poetic works like *Basavodaharanam* of the Vaishnava poets of the 9th century rendered in the name of their deity, Basava.

---

[1] *Sahabhavana*, in **Gaana Kusumaalu**, Vijayawada: 2002, p. xiv.

[2] *Abhinandanalu*, in **Gaana Kusumaalu,** Vijayawada: 2002, p.vii.

The next writing of Dr. Raj in Telugu, *Kim Kartavyam* was a compilation of his *Yakshagaana* compositions (classical dance dramas), the most popular piece bearing the title of the book. There are five such compositions in all in this book. Another of his writings, *Veda Vinodini* (Scriptural Amusement) is a unique creation with the last line of each stanza posing a riddle from the vast expanse of Biblical stories, and the answer is to be filled in the preceding three lines of the stanza. One example goes like this:

> Problem – The light that a wise man could not see, an ass had seen!

> Solution – Humans sometimes cannot see the ways of God – like Prophet Bilam could not see the light ahead, but his ass could see.

This work is a *Sataka* (a composition of a hundred or more poems) as well, with a difference! It is a unique literary exercise in Christian literature presenting good humor and amusement in the acquisition of Biblical knowledge.

The latest composition in Telugu is the book under present consideration, entitled *Gaana Kusumaalu* (Song Flowers). The English rendering of this composition is entitled 'Geetha Malika' (Garland of Song Flowers). There are 44 songs in all in this book and each one is a master piece with both literary value and theological import. The present English edition contains alternative renderings for some of the songs, which are given in the Appendix with the respective serial numbers. As the author himself says, most of these songs or hymns were written over three decades ago. And this attests to the fact that they have stood, and stood well, the test of time! Some of them had become very popular as they were first sung by professional artistes and broadcast on Voice of the Gospel Christian radio (*Suvartha Vaani*). Almost every cross section of the Telugu Christian populace around the world used to sing some of them, though most of them never knew who wrote these famous and familiar songs. A cassette with the title *'Pasidikanthulu'* (The Golden Rays) was produced by St. Luke's Lalit Kala Ashram with 8 songs from the book in 1970's. The author in his preface to *Gaana Kusumaalu* tells of another cassette of 8 songs with the title *Premajyothi Yesu Gaana Kusumaalu* (Song Flowers of Jesus, the Light of Love) which was not available to the present reviewer. It was learnt that it was released about the same time. An MP3 CD entitled *'Golden Hits of Rev. Dr. P. Solomon Raj'* with forty five songs was released by Prabhudeva Ministries in Vijayawada on the 60th Wedding Anniversary of the author in 2006. Some 28 songs from the book were included in the CD, while there are 11 new compositions. Some 5 of the songs from the book are presented with old tunes as well as with a new tune.

All these songs in the book and those new ones in the CD are as fresh in depth and meaning today as when they were written. This freshness may be accounted for by the subject matter being woven around the eternal message of the Scriptures; and this sustains them to bring lessons for all times and climes. And this work is a culmination of Bhakti flowing through the twin stream of *sahitya* and *sangeetha* – beautiful verse put in melodious tune – refreshing many a wearied soul as they sing or listen to these songs!

INTRODUCING 'GEETHA MALIKA'

Often we see that writings translated into other languages from the original lose their original tempo and tenor. But we don't have such a problem with the present work, since it is rendered from Telugu into English by the author himself. The author had been at phenomenal ease in presenting almost each of his artistic creations with a matching verse – superb in diction and profound in meaning. For me, he is a born poet, with inborn skills of poetic aptitude and imagination. Added to this was his incessant *saadhana* in the realms of art and poetry, which had placed him and his works on higher pinnacles of almost global reputation.

The scope of the present essay confines our attention to the theological themes of his present work. Before we launch the exciting exercise through his 44 steps up on his *Bhakti yaatra* (devotional pilgrimage), which may be called *'Songs of Solomon'*, it is appropriate to note that he dedicated this *Geetha Malika* (Garland of Song Flowers) to his beloved parents. This is a token of his *'honor your father and mother'* - expressed in verse. He was proud of his father (who died in the author's childhood). He lived as an ideal school teacher – a versatile genius with a multifaceted personality:

A friend of the young and old,

A voice to the voiceless,

A valiant leader who declared

There should be no neglected soul in the society.

As a grateful tribute, he writes, "To his memory I offer these humble lines, As a garland from a grateful son".

Recalling the Biblical character after whom his mother was named, he extols his mother who had a great impact not only on him but also upon countless rural folks of the times:

Naome is also the name

Of the woman who gave birth to me.

She was named after the blessed woman in the Bible.

She in her turn became the teacher and guide to

Countless poor women in our land,

Wherein is flowing the river Godavari;

> She became a widow herself,
>
> I remember her with a thankful heart.

This is an acknowledgment that he owes his greatness to the godly upbringing by his parents within their limited means.

MAJOR THEMES IN THE 'SONGS OF SOLOMON RAJ'

The major theological themes dealt with in these *bhakti geetas* (devotional songs) pertain to the author's views on God the Father, Christology and Christian eschatology. An analytical study of these themes in the light of the songs in this book will be attempted in this essay. The scope of the present essay takes us on an explorative and hopefully exciting walk through his hymns. It is hoped that this exercise will enable us to appreciate the richness and ethos of some of his theological thought. His Theological Proclamations, as mentioned above, are woven mainly around his conception about the Father God, the Incarnate Son, and the hope of glory at the end of life's journey. His strong belief in the triune God was expressed in the first two themes above, and his intimate relationship with God through his life's journey seems to have produced an unwavering assurance in His unending care at the end of life – as we see in these songs.

The very first song of the book entitled *'The Destiny'* beautifully encompasses these three themes with rich Indian imagery.

The Father God

Jesus has introduced the immortal, eternal and transcendental God as 'Our Father who is in heaven' making Him immanent to the mortals on earth. Solomon Raj begins his song with the words, 'O, our Father, God in heaven' confessing simultaneously His immanence as found in 'our Father' and at the same time His transcendence expressed in the words,

'God in heaven'. The transcendence of God is further expressed at the very outset as follows:

> And the blessed divine,
>
> Lord of all creation
>
> The highest God covered with
>
> The raiment of eternal glory
>
> Adored by Seraphim and Cherubim...

Such a transcendental God, at the same time, is approachable and befriendable as experienced and expressed by the author in a 'We-Thy' relationship: '*We* chant *thy* sacred name'.

The Incarnate Son

The Incarnation of Jesus Christ was possible not merely due to the will of the Father God but also because of the willingness of the Incarnate Son, who chose to empty Himself (the first two persons of the Godhead working together in undivided consultation with each other and with the Holy Spirit). The author extols the Incarnate Son as He rejected His glorious state ('*mahimaasthali*') in order to be born into this world and show the way for humans to find a deathless destiny:

> You, to become incarnate on this earth,
>
> Have never chosen to cling on to the glory
>
> Which You had with the Father.

The ultimate mission of the Incarnation was well expressed:

> ...You cleared the way
>
> For us to reach the realms of
>
> The deathless worlds.

We find beautiful Indian imagery when the author seeks the Lord's help to enable him continually praise Him:

In the blessed vicinity

Of Your lotus feet.

Help us to live there nourished on the sweet nectar

Of the endless song of Your praise.

The 'lotus feet' is a beautiful picture that describes the feet of God which have refuge-worthiness for a devotee. Lotus in Sanskrit is *'padma'* and is a symbol of purity in the midst of filth, primarily representing beauty and non-attachment. Having its roots in the mud it floats on the water without ever becoming wet or muddy. Above all other religious symbolism, the author obtains a new revelation from the lotus as it was suggestive of the resurrection of Christ and of the believer. The Loyola Press, a Jesuit Ministry, in an article on their web page entitled *'Examples of How Jesus Has Been Pictured Throughout History'* clearly presents the depth of the meaning of the imagery of lotus in the art of Dr. P. Solomon Raj:

> The lotus moves from the dark clay at the foot of the water and rises into light toward the sun. This is the message of the Gospel. At the bottom of the image is the demon of death. Christ is shown rising triumphantly and trampling the demon of death, who is virtually under his feet. Raj borrows this symbolism from Hindu iconography, which often shows the god figures trampling miniature forms of the demon of death or the demon of darkness.[3]

The imagery of 'lotus' is used several times in the 'Songs of Solomon Raj' as it meant much to the author. In *'The Love Song'* (Song No. 8), the author extolling the purpose of the Incarnation, expresses his desire to touch His blessed 'lotus' feet in adoration:

---

[3] *'Examples of How Jesus Has Been Pictured Throughout History'*, The Loyola Press. http://www.loyolapress.com/how-jesus-has-been-pictured-throughout-history.htm

To sing the song of love,

To feed on the showers of Your mercy dew,

To touch Your blessed lotus feet in adoration,

Lord, You have shown me the way.

Again, in the Song (No. 23), *'The Three Kings of the East'*, the author identifies himself with the Wise Men and brings body and mind to offer at His 'holy lotus feet':

For us to bring to You our body and mind

To offer them to You at Your holy lotus feet

With these our gifts to make devotion

And to ask in return Your endless blessing.

In the Song (No. 42) *'I am a Deer'*, the author again calls Him 'the Lord of the lotus feet' :

When I run away from the foes

I shall tell Him all my woes

And the Lord of the lotus feet

Will all my needs then meet.

The Hope of Glory at the End of Life's Journey

Dr. Raj, in his songs, beautifully and bountifully expresses his strong faith and hope in *'the realms of the deathless worlds'*, and *'regions where there are no tears'*:

While we walk on the earth, Lord,

Where there is no solace to our souls,

Do Thou shed upon us Your shalom

Till at the end we stand with You

In the regions where there are no tears.

When the pilgrimage on this earth

Comes to its end.

When all is said and done, he invokes God, whom he describes as the 'Ocean of Love', to come and receive with His outstretched arms into heaven's haven of life and comfort on the last leg of life's journey. Ocean is a familiar Oriental image for endless and fathomless love of God. With an unshakable trust in the Lord, Who is preparing mansions for His beloved, the author expresses the anticipation of the faithful and seeks His help at the end of our *'walk on the earth'*:

> Come Lord to us to stretch Your hand,
>
> And receive us to Your home, the deathless land.
>
> This we ask You, O God incarnate.

These three themes above are artistically and skillfully interwoven throughout the 'Songs of Solomon'.

The fourth song entitled **'Praise the Lord'** is another example of a classical song in which all these major themes are embedded. God is portrayed as 'holy and adorable' Creator, Who, in the beginning 'through the work of his Son',

> Made the earth and all the creatures therein
>
> Also the sun the moon and the stars in heaven
>
> And the various seasons for our good.
>
> He also
>
> ...made with great love nights and days,
>
> The seasons of the earth,
>
> The rain and wind.

It is amazing that such all-powerful Creator 'called us His dear children'. When "the humankind has left His paths, Tempted by sin and earned His curse', it was

> He who broke the bondage of Death
>
> And had destroyed the thorn of Death

And saved the earth while it was groaning in pain

And in endless misery ...

The author then talks about the Son as follows:

Our Lord Jesus Christ, to wipe away our sin and the curse

To make us holy and to heal the scars of our transgression,

Became incarnate and the earth rejoiced.

... the blessed Savior

Who died for us on the cross and rose again from the dead.

The creedal confession about the Lord is aptly and appropriately expressed in the above lines. Finally the author praises the Holy Spirit, Who is the 'Lord and comforter,

Who makes us wise in life and leads us along the way

Guiding us now with none else to lead

... no one else to save ...

Thus one can see a reflection of the Apostles' Creed in this song. In the original song in Telugu, there is a clear mention of the author's hope of glory when he writes on Jesus the heavenly Savior. Jesus is seen as the only adequate one to take us to His own abode on the last day (*'tudi dinamandu tanadagu neravu jerpaga jaaluvaadu'*). It was learnt that the stanza on the Holy Spirit was not sung in the original record by the cine artiste, and that only the script of the sung part was given in the book.

AN ANALYTICAL SURVEY OF THE 'SONGS OF SOLOMON RAJ'

The above three-fold themes have interspersed throughout the songs, and the author had skillfully woven most of his songs around these foundational doctrines of our faith and experience. An analytical survey of these songs, with the undergirding themes, may be attempted as follows:

1. THE FATHER GOD

The Song (No. 18) on *'The Creation'* is a *'Bhajan'* song based on Psalm 90. Some of the divine attributes of God are beautifully portrayed in this Song:

> O, Lord, our King and our God,
>
> You alone are our shelter
>
> From generation to generation   ...

The lines given below form the Chorus confessing the relationship with such a Creator God, which is repeated at the end of each stanza; this is one of the distinct features of *'Bhajan'*. And this refrain talks of an eternal relationship 'for ages and ages' and 'from generation after generation':

> Before the hills were ever made,
>
> Before the earth was given its shape,
>
> For ages and ages, You have been our God;
>
> From generation to generation, You are our Lord.

The author at the end of the Song gives a note as to how it all goes in singing:

> This is typical *bhajan*. Line after line the first four lines of every stanza are repeated by a group as one person leads. At the end of the fourth line the leader and the followers all join singing the four lines of the refrain together. And the next stanza starts and goes on as before.

The wonder of His creation and the vanity of mortal life is depicted in the following stanzas:

> O, God, You will beckon us to Your side
>
> As our mortal abodes go into the clay   ...

Like the green grass that sprouts in glory at dawn,

The human kind flourishes by Your grace for an hour.

But soon, in the next hour

They wither away and droop to the earth.

In the light of this revelation and awareness, the author makes a prayer at the end for grace to be wise stewards of life:

Lord, teach us to fear You,

And lead us with You in the paths of life.

Give us grace to serve You while we live

And receive us at the end into the realms where You live.

2. THE INCARNATE SON

Almost three-fourths of the Songs deal with the theme of the Incarnate Son, touching various dimensions of the Incarnation – such as His name, His birth, His crucifixion, His resurrection, and one's walk with the Lord.

A. On His Name

In the Song (No. 19) on *'The Name of Jesus'* the author praises the Name of Jesus which is 'sacred'. This Song in Telugu had a special significance in that it had been chosen as the Andhra Pradesh Convention[4] Song for 1974. With fitting tune and profound meaning, the Song became very popular, and is being used in churches till today. This Song is also included in the Andhra Christian Hymnal (Song No. 699).[5] It declares that Jesus is the way, 'the only way' to everlasting life. And,

---

[4] Andhra Pradesh Conventions were the biennial conventions held at Krishna River bank in Vijayawada by the Andhra Christian Council, for Telugu Christians of all denominations in the State.

[5] 2008 edition, published by Prabodha Book Centre, Vijayawada.

For the remission of the sins of humanity

For us to see the other side of life's journey

And cross the ocean of death

Jesus is the only way.

The Name of Jesus is sacred as He "Has laid down His life as gift unparalleled, Forgiving us our dreadful sins with mercy, He stretched His hand to give us shelter". Having risen from death 'to give us His own life' ... He 'Gave to us His own name'. Being our eternal contemporary,

Today our King and Keeper stands with us

As we walk our way along with Him

We sing praises all the way to Him

Till we become one with Him.

In the Song (No.28) *'The Ray of Hope'* the Lord is shown as 'the hope of our ancient fathers' and so a prayer is offered to Him:

Lead us through the deathless path

So that we may keep looking at You

And attain the land of peace at the end.

Once our fathers walked in paths of tribulation

They never lost hope, in their hearts

But with great courage and faith

They walked ahead and reached their goal.

There is a mention of the 'paths of tribulation' through which 'our fathers walked'. This might very well be the social isolation and ostracism of the ancient times. The author must have been aware of the debilitating impact of caste system and the evil of untouchability of those bygone days. And he recollects how the predecessors had withstood the onslaught of social evils, and had persevered to see a new day 'where the mind is without fear, and the head is held high'! The author identifies with the precious faith of his fathers in the above lines. In conclusion, he presents the picture of the prophetic vision when all creatures live together in harmony: [6]

> O, ray of hope, You're the power of God.
>
> You lead all people in Your fearless path,
>
> Till the rulers of this earth bow down before You,
>
> And all creatures live under the rule of love.

B. On His Birth

'The Love Song' (Song No. 8) envisages the purpose of the divine Incarnation:

> To quench the flames of sin and curse,
>
> To help to cast away the dread of death,
>
> Lord, You have died on the cross
>
> And have showed me the way.
>
> To give us the gift of eternal life,
>
> And to bring peace to the whole earth,
>
> Lord, You became incarnate
>
> And showed us the way.

Christ's Crucifixion is mentioned before the Incarnation in the above song. This may be to emphasize the purpose of the Incarnation – He was born to die! It was Bob Mumford who reminded that the cross was in the heart of God from the beginning, which was graphically seen in the very structure of the camp of the people of Israel during their journey in the wilderness. An aerial view of the camp of the different tribes,

---

[6] Isaiah 65:25.

whenever and wherever they halted, clearly looked like a cross, which was a gentle reminder to God the Father of the inevitability of the Cross in 'the fullness of time'.[7]

In the Song (No.9) **'The Morning Star'**, the author addresses the Morning Star, the Star of Bethlehem, and pleads it five times at the end of most of the stanzas :

Caste out the darkness and show us the way ...

Lead us on till we draw near

The crib where Jesus our Lord does lay.

The author then talks about the King, Whose birth the star points to, and Who had condescended Himself. It's all done in the third person singular in the third stanza :

The King who created all the worlds

Is sleeping in the little manger as a baby;

He who rules the heavenly realms

Has come down to be born on this earth.

In the fourth stanza also the author talks about Him in the third person singular:

To Him we cannot offer gold and frankincense,

Nor can we give all the pearls of the oceans as gift,

Since all the diamonds of the earthly mines are already His,

So we offer Him but our hearts and worship with joy.

Thinking or talking about Him in a meaningful way, though in the third person, must have brought the author all of a sudden into the very presence of the Lord, wherein he could

---

[7] See *Spirit-Filled Life Bible* for a diagram of the cross with relevant details. p. 193.

not but talk to Him personally in an intimate 'I-Thou' relationship:

It is not possible, Lord, to offer gifts to You

Nor to try and earn Your favor ever,

So I give my heart to You and worship, my Lord

And become Your slave all through my life.

In the Song (No. 10) *'My Eyes Do Glow'* the author testifies, 'my eyes glow with joy' because of the Incarnation of Jesus:

He left His heavenly home

To seek and save the sinners,

To give abundant life to human race;

And therefore my eyes glow with joy.

To fulfill God's great promise to us,

The glorious Lord and the true Word

Came down to the earth as one like us;

And therefore my eyes glow with joy.

In the last stanza, he extends his worship 'in grateful adoration' and rejoices in the mystery of incarnation:

To Jesus who is born on this earth

To the Lord who has pitied our plight.

The Song (No. 15) *'Descent from Heaven'* is another lyric on the wonder of the Incarnation of Jesus Christ:

O maker and the ruler of the universe

You deemed to live with us?

As He made His dwelling among us, the author wonders how He transforms us:

... As Your glorious grace shines on our race

Making our paths aglow with Your rays

You scattered the gloom from our lives.

The author finally makes a plea to the Lord to visit us once again:

To make the withering earth

Bloom again with Your life-giving light

Shed Your rays on us again

Lord to seek and save us.

In his preface to this book in Telugu, Karanam Balasubrahmanyam Pille aptly remarked about a particular line in the last stanza wherein the author invokes the Lord to visit us once again 'since we went astray from Your path': *'Daari tolagina mammunu veduka / Mariyokapari itu rave Deva'*.[8] This, Pille remarks, reminds us of the Lord's parable of the lost sheep wherein the incessant longing of the Good Shepherd for the lost is well described.

The Song (No. 16) **'The Blessed Incarnation'** is another lyric on the Incarnation of Jesus Christ. A beautiful invocation of the Incarnation is found in the Chorus:

O merciful Lord, adorable God

Robed in righteousness and Prince of peace

Jesus our King worshipped by the Universe.

The author ponders about the various facets of the blessing endowed upon humankind by the Incarnate Lord:

O Lord incarnate, giver of eternal life

... Son of God watching over the humankind.

------

[8] *Sahabhavana,* in **Gaana Kusumaalu**, Vijayawada: 2002, p. xiii.

... To fill the earth with endless peace

And take us home to Your heavenly realms ...

... To set to rest our woes on the earth

And to give us Your matchless inheritance

O Son of God healer and restorer ...

There's no wonder the author concludes:

'Who is there but You to show us the way?'

The Song (No. 21) *'The Abode of Our Lord'* portrays how life is transformed as one would 'approach the abode of my Lord':

My heart is lighted up with His light

My mind blooms like a flower

My foot becomes quick

As I approach the abode of my Lord.

Lighted heart, flower in bloom, and quickened foot are symbols of a new life in God. As the author sees this 'descent of the heavenly hosts, And the coming down of the glorious light', he rejoices: 'My heart becomes filled with His light'. And all this is possible because,

The King Himself stooped down to earth

And became a Babe in Bethlehem's inn ...

This is a deep experience like Isaiah the prophet saw in the vision.

The Song (No. 22) on *'The Baby Jesus'* is another song on the Incarnation of Jesus Christ. Jesus is twice acknowledged as 'The ruler of the heavenly realms'. The purpose of the Incarnation is expressed in unmistakable terms:

(He) Is born today to save us.

To lead us on the path not straying

And take us safely home.

In the last stanza, the author who witnesses 'The golden circle surrounding His head' – the nimbus we see in Christian art works - declares that it 'Is the great and glorious crown, To tell us that He is the King of kings'. The author, himself being an artist, here talks about the halo around the head of Jesus, signifying that He is indeed 'the ruler of the universe'!

The Song (No. 23) on ***The Three Kings of the East*** is another song on the Incarnation. The author graphically narrates the course the Kings of the East have taken in paying 'homage to the King of kings' and declaring 'Him as the heavenly King'. The author then goes a step forward in personal application:

> So that we may also seek You and find
>
> To see with our eyes the ocean of mercy...
>
> So that our feet may find the way
>
> And to follow Your path without mistake
>
> We too come to Thy lowly manger
>
> And kneel down like them to pay our homage ...

The author appropriately invokes personal devotion (*bhakti*) and takes the opportunity to worship the Lord and seek His perennial blessing:

> For us to bring to You our body and mind
>
> To offer them to You at Your holy lotus feet
>
> With these our gifts to make devotion
>
> And to ask in return Your endless blessing.

Dr. Raj tells us elsewhere the traditional story of the wonderful golden chest he saw in KÖLM Cathedral, wherein, people believe, the relics of the three wise men are kept.

The Song (No. 24) **'*A Light to Lighten the Earth*'** is another exercise of the author in portraying the outstanding blessings for humanity with the dawn of the Star of the Lord. The refrain sums up the whole message:

> As the brightest light shines in the sky
>
> The gloom of the earth was cast away.

'The thickest night and the blindening darkness' not only 'Melted down as the ray shined in people's eye' but their very 'countenance went aglow'. The author further points out the liberating impact of 'the newest song of the Savior's love':

> The broken hearts of the oppressed race
>
> Got redeemed from nagging doubt and great despair
>
> ...
>
> The fear of death has been driven away.

The theme of 'liberation' appears in several ways in Dr. Raj's art works too.[9]

The night that brought a total transformation to the destiny of humans is well described in another Song (No. 31) entitled *'The Holy Night'*. In four stanzas, the author describes what happened when Jesus was born - on the earth, in the skies, in Mary's heart, and to the destinies of humans:

> ...   Silence ruled the whole creation
>
> When God Himself became a man and was born on the earth.
>
> A great star   ...   in the sky
>
> Hosts of angels came down to earth
>
> To sing praises and wake up men
>
> When our Lord Jesus came as a baby.

---

[9] *'Liberation in Luke's Gospel'* by Dr. P. Solomon Raj contains 12 woodcuts on liberation from 12 different maladies – all from Luke's Gospel with matching meditations.

> ... The mystery still lingered in her mind
>
> The Holy Spirit still ruled in her heart
>
> When the baby Jesus slept in the manger.
>
> But the darkness of sin has fled in flight
>
> The curse on mankind rolled away then
>
> The presence of God to be with the earth
>
> When God Himself came down to the earth.

Jesus is portrayed as *'The Son of Man'* in this Song (No. 29); yet, He is called: 'Merciful Lord, conqueror of death, The way of life and Savior divine'. For this reason, he prays to Him: 'Show Your mercy and save us, Lord! In the second stanza, the author envisages the meaning in terms such as – incarnation, death on the cross, and cleansing from His blood:

> For us humans You came to the earth
>
> You died on the cross and rose again
>
> By the blood which flowed from Your side
>
> You cleanse us from our sins, O Lord!

Finally, in view of the incidence of sin and the resultant curse and death, the author praises the Lord for what He has done:

> O Lord of love and treasure to the earth
>
> You opened the gates of eternal life!

In the Song (No. 37) *'The Lord of the Children'* the author portrays how the children identify with the Incarnate Son of God, Jesus. They call Him their 'companion', their 'everlasting friend', their 'commander' and their 'ruler'. They also have Him as 'the leader on the earth leading us', 'the wayfarer walking with us here', 'the master showering His blessings' and as the one who 'shows us the path of righteousness'. They have a solid base for such an intimate relationship with Him:

The Kingdom of God is of the little ones

Let them come to Me, He said.

Who is that blessed Lord Who laid His hands

To bless us, and hugged us with love?

The Song (No. 39) *'Nativity'* is another masterpiece on the Incarnation of Jesus Christ, and the beauty of the Incarnation is pictured here in a new imagery.

> ...　Was born in the manger the Savior, our Lord
>
> The incarnation of the Logos and the Son of God.
>
> ...　Indeed He came to the earth as God's greatest gift
>
> To reconcile God to man and stop the rift.
>
> To redeem the humanity from death He came
>
> Son of God and Son of Man and Savior is His name
>
> Of the womb of Mary the blessed Mother, thrice virgin
>
> Immanuel, that is God with us, humble, loving and lowly.

The idea of Mary being 'thrice virgin' comes to Dr. Raj from Eastern Orthodox icons and their theology. They wanted to emphasize the particular doctrine that Mary had no other children. The artists, when they made the picture of *Mater Theo* (Mother of God), put three stars on her image to suggest that she was virgin before, during, and after the birth of Jesus Christ. Dr. Raj, however, is not thinking of that doctrine here.

Finally, the author elucidates the purpose of the Incarnation again and makes a grand proclamation:

> ... to win the deadly fight
>
> And reach the heavenly realms ...
>
> And by His advent to the earth He has driven our fears away.

The darkness of ignorance has fled in His mighty light

The heavenly Guru by His light has put our fear to flight
And He beckoned us to join and walk with the heavenly
hosts

Till at the end we ever live with the Father, Him and
the Holy Ghost.

The author beautifully affirms the doctrine of Trinity in this
song, when he states at the end that we 'ever live with the
Father, Him and the Holy Ghost'.

An alternative rendering of the Song (No. 39) is *'The
Brilliant Baby'*. The purpose of the Incarnation is beautifully
enunciated in this Song. Jesus, 'the matchless image of the
glorious Creator' is also portrayed as 'the great forgiver ':

... Then was He born in the manger, the baby our
Lord

And He lighted the universe.

The matchless image of the glorious Creator

And to the sinning humans the great forgiver

Came to bear our sins.

The author portrays how the 'Desire of Ages' further 'came
to the earth as God's great gift':

Those who awaited for many generations to see the
Savior

Have today praised God in a thousand tongues for His
favor

And ... to grant the eternal life to humans destined
to death,

The source of life today as a little baby came to the earth

As God's great gift.

He Himself to lift us from the curse of sinful grave

Came down with love for us to redeem and save

And He took upon Himself our burdens.

...   Was born to carry on His shoulders the curse of sin

And came to give us heavenly gifts.

Sent as 'God's great gift', He not only 'came to give us heavenly gifts' but also 'to declare the day of redemption':

That the people of the earth will cross the ocean of grief

And stand in God's presence finding in Him relief

He foretold His coming to His people

To take us ... where there is no shedding of tears

To declare the day of redemption and to wipe away our tears.

'A Light to the Gentiles' (Song No. 40) is another song on the event of the Incarnation. The transforming impact of the Incarnation on the whole creation is aptly expressed:

The earth became lighted up

Death itself became mortal.

Curse moved away

As God became man in the womb of Mary.

The two-fold purpose of the Advent of Christ is seen in the following lines in that it affects both the life on earth and the life after death:

To save the earth from peril

And to redeem the Adam's race

With immeasurable mercy

He came to abide with us.

... For us to walk on the deathless path

He gave His likeness to the mortals.

In this song, Dr. Raj remembers the story of St. Francis of Assisi who is said to have made the first crib with twigs and leaves to celebrate the birth of Christ.

'The Song of the Angels' (Song No. 41) is based on the most familiar passage of Scriptures on the birth of Jesus Christ. The twin purpose of the Incarnation, sung by the angels, reverberates in this song:

Glory to God in the highest,

And Peace and well being

To God's blessed ones on the earth.

The refrain singing 'Glory to God in the highest' at the end of each stanza not only adds beauty to the song, but also gives a reason to glorify God. The words of this song, with which the angels announced the birth of Jesus, are heard today in all languages of the earth, where God's people worship Him in many languages.

The Son of God came to the earth

To bear our heavy loads...

The very Son of God drove out the darkness

So the world may not be caught

In the terrible darkness of sin...

He fed those who came to Him hungry

And sent away the proud with empty hands.

In the three stanzas (*charanams*) of this song, the author gives three distinct reasons for ascribing 'Glory to God in the highest' in a fitting manner.

C. On His Crucifixion

The Song (No. 5) *Eternal Life Flowing out of the Cross,* is a panegyric on the riches of the cross. In this song, the author poses six typically different questions in each of the first six stanzas, the answer for all being an emphatic 'NO'. But in the last stanza, we see a resounding 'YES' as an ultimate 'ANSWER' to all the 'NO's' of life – all because of the cross! Though 'the way of the cross is sorrowful', the author writes,

...   only there can we find

The water of life to quench our thirst,

And the life force to restore our dying souls.

This ultimate answer in the cross satisfies all the following questions the author very searchingly posed in each stanza of this song:

... Where is the ray to brighten our path?

Where is the song to make our hearts glow?

...   Where do we find waters to quench our thirst?

And save us from the dread of parching death?

...   Where is the bloom to sooth our tired body?

And where is the healing wind to our sickened soul?

...   Where are the soothing wasps of wind to cool our hearts

 And to renew our hope?

...   Where is the possible shelter?

Wherein to hide our heads?

...   Where do we find a little light,

To lead our steps slowly along the way?

The poet here makes strange and contrasting pairs like ray of hope in blindening darkness, waters in the paths of dry rock, balm to cure the bite of the venomous viper, et cetera. This seems to be his way of showing joy and redemption through the painful cross. This song reminds us of the contrasts in St. Francis' prayer – 'Lord, make me an instrument of Your peace'.

'The Pillar of Sacrifice' (No. 26) is another song on the Cross of Christ, expounding all that it had wrought for the humans. The chorus points the listeners to the premises of crucifixion, and they are enabled to ponder the miracles done through the 'cross experience' of the 'Lamb of God' as ennumerated in each of the five stanzas :

In the world   ...   cursed with sin

And where it was thrown in the abyss of death

There dear Jesus ...

Laid His life and died on the cross ...

Outside the city walls and by the wayside sun

In the scorching day light in the terrible noon

In agony which no one had ever did suffer

He died for us and yet He lives forever ...

For us the sinning and helpless souls

He came down even from the heavenly realms

Through His death to give us heavenly bliss

And bring to us God's forgiveness ...

To the helpless creatures seeking in vain

The living waters in dried up wells

He came to bring us to God again

And to bliss with which He always fills ...

When the human race went astray and missed the path

And became blind and merited God's wrath

Jesus our Lord brought His great salvation

And between God and man a great reconciliation.

D. On His Resurrection

In *'The Resurrection Song'* (No. 12) the author enunciates the purpose of the resurrection of Jesus Christ from the dead in simple but profound terms :

He has risen from the dead   ...

To give us life and from death to save

Now and forever that life is ours in deed.

Though this is basically a 'Resurrection Song', the author loses no opportunity to envisage the purpose of His Incarnation :

He brought us to the Father's realms

By His blessed Incarnation

He has broken the curse of our sin

So we all can inherit heaven.

Finally he extols the uniqueness of Jesus on account of His atoning sacrifice, and victory over sin and death:

Where else we find a blessed One like Him

Who put down His life for us humans?

None but our Lord Jesus Christ alone,

Who could make our transgressions atone,

Is the victor over sin and the conqueror of death.

Another Song (No. 14) on the Resurrection of Jesus Christ is *'Sing with the Conqueror'*. The author in deed affirms this event in history as a 'wonderful story filled with glory' and this note rings out at the end of every stanza and dispels every fear. In the second stanza, the author extols the cross and all that was wrought by it for humankind :

> For people to cross the endless abyss
>
> For humans to reach the glory and the bliss
>
> He laid down His life
>
> And ended the strife.

The last two stanzas are full of imagery. The following lines liken the glorious event of resurrection to 'a wonderful bloom, Spreading around His great perfume' - as Jesus rose up discarding the mortal body. In the last stanza, we see the picture of the *'sleeping worm'* (Chrysalis) which wakes up in turn, 'Breaking the prison' wherein it lied dormant before. And this, he says, is the reason for rejoicing:

> He rose again to life and has ended the strife
>
> Therefore we sing and the ends of earth will ring.

E. On Walking with the Lord

There are many songs in the book (about one fourth in the Book) which portray the Incarnate Son and the author's intimate relationship with Him. We will see the second and third songs in the book now, which are taken from the author's **'Kim Kartavyam'**. In the Song (No. 2) **'O Son of Mary'**, the author addresses Jesus as 'Lord Jesus, Son of Mary'. He sees Him as 'matchless Light' and pleads Him, 'Have mercy on us'. 'Son of Mary' is an expression not so frequently used in the Protestant literature in India. But like the title, 'Son of Man' used by Christ Himself, 'Son of Mary' here is an expression of the humanity of Christ, as the well known term 'Son of God' tells us about the divinity of Christ. The author freely used that epithet here, but demonstrates his distinctive faith by pleading Him directly for His mercy. In all this, he seems to be emphasizing the humanity of Jesus, yet he acknowledges His divinity by saying, "We bow our heads before Your ever shining Countenance". In the next stanza he amply admits the divinity of Jesus:

O, Lord God, abiding in matchless light,

Ever surrounded by the adoration

Of the heavenly hosts,

Glorious Incarnation and worshipful Lord,

Help us to see your blessed Countenance.

The author closes this song with beautiful Biblical imagery of 'the vine and the branch' as he expresses his intimate 'I-Thou' relationship with the Incarnate Lord and pleads for His mercy to abide with Him and shine for Him:

You are the vine and I the branch

To abide with You and always live

Bearing fruits and shine for You

Give me that grace, O merciful One.

In the Song (No.3) *'Prayer of the Woman of Samaria'*, the author presents a three-fold confession of the Samaritan woman: First, about her ignorance - that she did not know Him and discern His ways though He was 'declared to us by the Holy Scriptures' and was 'full of glory and the essence of all the Scriptures'; Second, about the futility of her quest - that she 'became thirsty and wandered around broken cisterns' to quench her thirst; Third, about her life's fulfillment - 'I find rest to my bruised body, I find now the living waters of life, While all along I was among the broken cisterns'. Here is an allusion to the Biblical account of the people of God hewing them out 'broken cisterns' without turning to 'the fountain of living water'.[10] All this pitiable plight of humankind was beautifully portrayed in this song in response to her oft-repeated prayer: 'Have mercy on me'! The original title to Jesus in Telugu version of the hymn is deep in meaning. He is called *Nigama Vedya,* meaning One Who was announced in ancient Scriptures.

In the Song (No. 11) *'The Anniversary'* the author describes the determined walk of a disciple with Christ. The chorus is filled with thanksgiving and praise to the Lord "Who kept us, And guided us along the way ... our guide and keeper". As a response of gratitude at the milestone of every New Year, now comes the pledge for a walk with Him:

We walk with Him leaving the old behind,

We cast our cares on Him to bear for us;

We know that this is a new way and a new path

And we go forward with Him with a new hope and joy.

...   We know this is a new path for us with Him

And ask the Lord to keep us from temptation.

We've decided to walk with Him and never to turn back,

We will not lay down the banner from our hand;

We run forward without ceasing

And tell others that it is a good day.

The Song (No. 13) *'The Living Waters'* also is about one's walk with the Lord. It is written in a classical literary style, the author speaking to himself about the futility of searching

---

[10] Jeremiah 2:13.

for living waters in places apart from Christ. In the chorus and the four stanzas of this song, the author states different queries and asks himself to consider them. Here are some questions posed for personal reflection:

Why do you seek water, my soul,

In the dried up wells? ...

In broken cisterns, my soul?

This is an expression of vain search for eternal joy in the wrong places. There are some bold proclamations made about Jesus in this song:

Jesus our Lord alone is the never drying spring

To quench your thirst and give the fill, my soul!

... But only Jesus the blessed Son of God

Can shower His mercy and quench our endless thirst.

This song has a similar pattern as one in the Telugu hymnal, *'Yesuni premanu nemarakanu yeppudu dalachave yo manasa'*[11] (Meditate upon the love of Jesus, O, my soul, without forgetting).

The Song (No. 20) *'A Child's Prayer'* is about children's walk with the Lord. Children have a sure opportunity for identifying with Jesus, since they celebrate His birth every year with joy, and they are taught that He loved and received the children without hindering them anytime. So children too can come boldly into the presence of the Lord with confidence and this Song is such a beautiful exercise:

With You we hold our hands, Lord

And walk along the way.

---

[11] *Andhra Christian Hymnal,* Song No. 173 by Dorasami Arogyam.

> Our God, You fill our life with Your gifts
>
> And do not caste us away Your dear ones
>
> O Jesus Who once walked this earth
>
> As a little one like one of us.

The children having an 'I-Thou' relationship with the Lord is wonderful; and for them to approach Him since He 'once walked, As a little one like one of us' is beautiful. They walk with Him and talk with Him as their friend. Even in their faltering mumblings and tumbling steps the children seem to be conscious of a 'companion':

> As we take our slate and stylus to learn to write
>
> As we walk the earth with faltering steps
>
> Night and day as a companion
>
> You walk with us we pray, our Lord.

With their innocence and honesty they pledge their lives to walk with the Lord, and to 'walk with righteousness':

> As we walk with You with hearts free from sin
>
> Following Your footprints true and faithful
>
> We walk with righteousness, Our Lord
>
> And remain Your true children in deed.

'A Child's Covenant' (No. 27) is another song that talks about the children's walk with the Lord in a covenant relationship. Though they are 'little children' they see themselves as 'soldiers of Christ' making a pledge with a sincere commitment:

> We walk ahead holding His cross in our hands
>
> To conquer the evils of the earth
>
> And to win the war against Satan.

Their obedience to 'the call of the Lord' help them 'walk faithfully with Him':

> To go along the righteous path
>
> And never ever to go astray.

Identifying themselves as 'the sheep of our Lord' they were assured of His unfailing providence. The imagery of Psalm 23 is skillfully reflected in the following lines:

> We shall never be in want
>
> We along the shores of living water
>
> Both day and night in His keeping.

The imagery of 'playmates in childhood' is applied to the children and Baby Jesus, and this gives them an opportunity to 'learn from Him mercy and love'. The author then uses the imagery of armor and soldiers in the last two stanzas to portray the commitment of children to the Lord:

> We wear the armor of righteousness
>
> And walk with Him in the holy path
>
> Holding fast in our hands
>
> The swiftest sword of His holy Word.

The imagery of the 'sword' is taken from the Pauline 'armor of God'.[12] We see that commitment to the Lord requires commitment to His Word – abiding by His Word! And then as 'warriors' of a new order, they stand out bold:

> We will never fear any foes
>
> And we shall abide in the blessed arms
>
> Of Him Who has conquered death.

In this hymn, we see Jesus as the Commander of 'little children, soldiers of Christ'. Referring to Christ, it is very rarely that this author talks about war, arms, and triumphant warrior

---

[12] Ephesians 6:11-17.

and ruler, much less as army commander. This song is an exception. To him a loving master is a more important image. But it is somewhat natural for children to use the heroic imagery in gentle terms sometimes; and so we have this one song in this tenor. There were a couple of hymns in the Hymnal with the same tenor – which were Telugu renderings from English: The hymn 'Onward Christian Soldiers' by Nabeen Barring-Gould was translated into Telugu by Jacob Chamberlane (Hymn No. 362). Another song, Stand Up, Stand Up for Jesus by George Duffield was translated by John Haye (Hymn No. 363). There was also an original song with popular tune, *'Yesuto ttheevigaanu podama'*, jointly authored by A. C. Kinsinger and P. D. Subhamani in almost the same tenor (Hymn No. 521). These songs which had been in vogue must have spurred Dr. Raj to pen the song under consideration.

In the Song (No. 32) *'The Refugee'* the author presents a superb piece of *Bhakti Sahitya* (devotional literature) which demonstrates the intimate 'I-Thou' relationship between a devotee and his God :

Who else but You

To save me and keep me, Lord?

No one but You is the gift-giver of life,

... I shall never forget You.

When I sought Your love

And came to You in faith

You without hiding Your face to me

Have beckoned me to Your bosom.

Even if my mother and father reject me

From You I get all I need

And You comfort me more than

My mother and father can do.

The first three stanzas above describe in intimate terms God's loving care for the devotee, and here is an acknowledgement of Christ as the only one Savior. God is given the epithet of 'gift-giver'. As the prophet Isaiah declared[13] God's care and comfort surpass those of a mother and father. The lyric ends with a deep desire that depicts the devotee's commitment to such a God:

I desire to abide with You

Both here and hereafter

I ask You to subdue my 'self'

And keep me ever in You.

The Song (No. 33) *'My Sole Refuge'* gives the key for union with God. It is nothing but the sacrifice of Jesus – His body broken for us, and His blood which is shed for us. The author extols Jesus as 'the giver of life', Who alone is his 'refuge' and Who will never leave him desolate. He further describes sustenance for life here and eternal life hereafter because of the supreme sacrifice of Jesus:

Your body of marvelous glory,

You have given to us for sustenance;

And the divine nectar is Your blood,

You gave so we receive to become deathless.

'Standing steadfast in the realms of faith' the author declares,

We worship You today without ceasing;

And conquer sickness and death,

And step forward with You in eternal joy.

---

[13] Isaiah 49:15.

Again the author expresses with fond anticipation:

> On the day when the eternal city
>
> Becomes our everlasting abode,
>
> When we rejoice in the never ending glory,
>
> We shall have the bliss of Your countenance.

The Song (No. 25) *'God's People'* is a call to the nation of Israel to turn to God 'And seek the shelter under the arm' since they had the assurance that the Lord 'will never forget His promises made to you'. The author further pleads the people of God to 'know the ways of His truth, And seek the strength of the Lord'; For,

> 'If humans seek Him His favor to show
>
> And return to ask His mercy now,
>
> He is ready to take pity again
>
> And show you again His salvation.

Finally, the author invites 'all the nations of the earth' to 'Gather around His mighty throne, Pay your homage and at His feet do fall, And worship Jesus Lord of all'.

The Song (No. 30), *'The Heart of Jesus'* demonstrates the author's anguish for people's dilemmas about Jesus. Citing different situations in the life of Jesus Christ, he wonders whether the people concerned know or understand the meaning of the Scriptures:

> Has this world ever known the heart of Jesus Christ?
>
> Has the human race ever seek the meaning of the
>
> Scriptures? ...
>
> Has the world really known the heart of Jesus?
>
> And has the human race sought to know the
>
> Scriptures?...

Have the people of the earth known the heart of Jesus?
And has the world ever understand the meaning of
the Scriptures?

Has the world tried to know the heart of Jesus?
And did the world know the meaning of the Scriptures?

Have the people known who Jesus really was?
And has the world known the meaning of the
Scriptures?

Did people understand what He was saying?
And did the world know that this is the fulfillment of
the Scriptures?

When Christ rose again from the grave and stood
In the midst of the disciples did they know that it was
true?

Having posed those different kinds of questions, the author
states a couple of staggering realities at the end:

Some people cannot see even if they have eyes to see!
And some people cannot hear even if they have ears to
hear!

The last Song (No. 44) in the book, *'The Disciples' Song'* is
taken from the author's song and dance drama, *Kim Kartavyam*,
but is a fitting finale for every disciple in his walk with the
Lord. It envisages the fulfilling experience of a disciple:

Lord our hearts are lighted

As we, Your great countenance behold.

Being overwhelmed by this, the disciple longs for unbroken
fellowship with the Lord in life and in eternity:

Can we ever forget You, our beloved?

And can we depart from Your blessed feet?

We do not want to go where You're not ;

With You we have all that we want.

...   You are the only One who pitied us and saved.

Open the doors of heavenly gates,

Send into our hearts Your breath to abide.

Have mercy, O Lord and leave us not,

And we steadfastly will cling on to Thee.

3. THE HOPE OF GLORY (AT THE END OF LIFE'S JOURNEY)

In the Song (No. 6) *'The Light in My Heart'* the author prays God to "Let the light in my heart, Glow brightly... To declare Thy path, And to people Thy word". He further pleads for God's help that he may go with God in full faith and to know 'the wonderful truth' which was 'revealed to our ancestors' and preserved for us in the Scriptures. Grace for the life's journey as seen above, and assurance of eternal bliss as given below are the two-fold concern of the author in this song:

At the advent of night

As life comes to close

Thy never-ending light

May be my repose

To keep me awake and never to fear

The thorn of death which pesters me here.

This will be my plea

... Thy glory to share

To live in the place where martyrs do stay

Keep singing Thy praise through the nightless day.

… the never-ending song.

The author longs for God's never-ending light to be his 'repose' at the end of life on earth. This he calls 'night' signifying the hope of resurrection that follows, since a new dawn always follows the night. And he longs to keep singing His praise in a 'never-ending song' throughout the deathless eternity, which is symbolically expressed as 'the nightless day'. Gandhiji loved the great hymn – 'Lead kindly Light' by Cardinal Newman. When he died, this is the song which Nehru suggested to sing at the funeral. Dr. Raj extols God in all the various renderings of this song as the 'Light in My Soul' or the 'Light in My Heart' and this is a well known and well sung lyric.

The author has done two other alternative renderings for this Song (No.6) and some distinctive thoughts are expressed therein. In the rendering entitled *'The Light in My Soul'* the author pleads with a yearning :

For in Thy path of love I go,

And that path to others I show.

Lord of life, You let them see

In my eyes Thy great mercy, the lamp of love.

And at the end, when darkness (of death) comes to hide his face, the author prays :

Keep me so I'm not afraid,

Teach me now to face the strife,

Help me O, the giver of life, the lamp of love.

When my journey comes to an end

And mine eyes seek the rest to find

In the land where there is no death,

And there will be my second birth, the lamp of love.

Stretch Your arm and gather my soul,

For all my woes at last to heal,

And firmly at Your blessed side

I shall forever and ever abide, the lamp of love.

Another rendering of this song (No. 6) **'Pray, Put a Flame of Light in My Heart'** is a two-fold prayer for both life on earth and life hereafter. With the revelation of God as the 'Lord of light' the author wastes no time but with a deep longing prays to God, Whom he calls 'Dear Lord'. This prayer for 'life on earth' reveals his consciousness of his mission of life, as well as the need for equipping himself for such a task:

> ...   let the flame in my heart brightly glow
>
> So I may give light to all people.
>
> Help me to walk in the paths of Your love
>
> And follow in the footsteps of the Lord of light
>
> So the world may see the light shining in my eyes.
>
> Lord, let the little flame in my heart brightly glow.

Concerning 'life hereafter' the author gently pleads the Lord for mercy that in his sun-set years of life he may experience God's sustaining grace and at the end that he be received by God into His Abode:

> When the evening of my earthly stay draws near,
> Receive me to Your bosom, O Lord,

I come casting behind all fears and all earthly loads
Have mercy on me, Lord, and save.

When the tiresome journey of this life is over,
And I close my eyes in soothing slumber,
Receive me to the deathless land and the nightless day
To the very place where You ever abide.

Philosophic Hinduism has much speculation about life after death. Dr. Raj is aware about the Upanishadic teaching of *Pithruloka* and *Devaloka,* the way of the sun light and of the cloud. So he is saying so much in these songs about the Biblical teaching of resurrection and eternal life.

In the Song (No. 37) *'The Lord of the Children'* the author portrays how the children identify with the Incarnate Son of God, Jesus, as He came of the virgin Mary,

Treading this earth like one of us little ones
The glorious Lord the Creator of this earth
...   Lord of life who conquered death.

The children talk of Him as their 'loving host' who gives them 'robes of righteousness and everlasting life'. They further demonstrate an unusual assurance of the future when none but the Lord takes them into His home:

When we finish the life's journey at the end
And reach our home.

In the Song (No. 38) *'Who Else but Jesus?'* the author portrays how the merciful Lord proves to be a faithful companion and comfort not only on life's journey but beyond:

Who is it who comes to hold my hand
As I breathe here my last?

Who is He that takes me home with Him?

Who else but Jesus my Lord - who died in my place,

And rose again to live forever?

4. OTHER THEMES

Finally, we see a couple of other themes the author deals with in these Songs, such as, life's pilgrimage, and, mission of life. A brief study of these is in order at this juncture:

A. Life's Pilgrimage

The Song (No. 17) *'The Pilgrim'* is an invitation for the pilgrim who is 'tired and broken hearted, And utterly lost'. The author extends a consoling conversation to the pilgrim, whose life grew weary, and whose journey had become dreary. Then he continues to minister encouragement to the pilgrim:

Just then the merciful Lord summons you to His side

And offers you the water of life

Therefore rejoice - And praise the Lord!

The author also addresses the questions the pilgrim confronts on the way and tries to ponder and communicate feasible answers:

As the Lord meets me on the way,

What are the signs by which I know?

And see Him as He is, you ask.

To know the Lord and see Him as He

There are marks of pierced nails in His feet

And prints of thorn wounds on forehead.

The unique identification marks of Jesus are presented beautifully and anyone can 'Look for them and see that it is He'. Again, the author raises another question concerning the utility of the search which might be racing in the mind of the pilgrim, and provides a reason enough for following Him:

If I see Him and follow Him walking along

What is it that I gain at the end?

Through the last lines the author proclaims a twofold deliverance from sorrow and pain, and a two-fold cover – all because of His mercy:

Yes the Lord of lords with mercy on you

Drives away your sorrow and your pain

And covers you with the ocean of His love

And keeps you forever.

Those who know the author remember that Dr. Raj had many trials, ups and downs in his life. This song indicates how he could cross the hurdles in his own life, looking at the Savior in Whom he put his faith.

In the Song (No. 38) **'Who Else but Jesus?'** the author portrays how the merciful Lord proves to be a faithful companion and comfort on life's journey:

... To quench my thirst

And give me solace?

... Who even now rules in my life?

Who is the God who makes me stand

In the heavenly realms -

Where there is the endless joy?

Who is the One who leads me on day by day ...

Wiping away the agonizing fear of guilt,

Bringing down the loads from my shoulders,

Who gives shelter to my helpless head?

Who is it who calls me to His bosom when I am tired?

To keep me company in my earthly journey

Not for a moment leaving me alone,

To put His merciful hand on my bruised head,

To carry all my woes and wipe away my tears ...

Who is adequate to help in all these daily chores on earth, the author declares:

'Who else is there but the Lord Jesus?

The Song (No. 42) *'I am a Deer'* is based on Psalm 42 and envisages the way for life's pilgrimage. The great affirmation of the Psalmist is reiterated in the chorus :

Like the deer thirsty for cool waters

So my heart gets thirsty for the love of my Lord.

The author extols the blessings of fellowship:

In the fellowship of that Lord

There is a feast to my heart ...

I will not find anywhere.

... 　By the shores of the clearest waters

My Lord in grace appears.

When He once comes near

There is no shadow of fear

Since He takes me to His side

And from danger surely will hide.

When I run away from the foes

I shall tell Him all my woes ...

> All my doubts and fears
>
> I shall now put in His ears
>
> My Lord ... Shall never send me in vain.

The author finally proclaims that He is unparalleled:

> Where else shall I get the peace?
>
> And where else my rest increase?
>
> Except with You my Lord ...

It is interesting to note that Dr. Raj presents his 42nd song with a similar note found in 42nd Psalm - which may not be a deliberate coincidence.

In *'The Song of the Flowers'* (Song No. 43), the author compares little children with flowers or flower plants. This is a beautiful image familiar to children in India. There are a few nursery rhymes in Telugu comparing children to flowers and flower buds.

> We are little tender flower plants
>
> We are lovely singing parrots ...
>
> We join each other our hands
>
> To say that we are truly friends
>
> We seek for a daily growing
>
> And pray for the Lord's blessing.

Unity and friendship are imperative for our existence, and a desire for consistent growth on a daily basis and prayer for the Lord's blessing are essential for existence on the planet Earth.

B. Mission of Life

God has a purpose for everyone whom He has created. To know it and flow in it brings fulfillment to life. God's purpose for our lives also includes making us His instruments to lead others to find their destiny. The Song (No. 7) *'The Story of the Little Lamp'* is a specimen to this. The author attains such a self-realization:

In the midst of the raging winds and the rising storm

The Lord has kept me like a lamp to shine.

... To cast away the darkness of the night

The Lord has kept me to shine.

.... There is no shadow ever to face

Where the Lord has kept me to shine.

With such a sense of life's vocation, he gives the call to the fellow travelers on life's journey to march forward without wavering on the way:

Behold it is the day break and no more night,

O, traveler, wake up and take thy staff,

Go walk in the lighted path,

Go forward, and why do you tarry?

In the Song (No.35) *'The Early Dawn'* the author enunciates in simple terms his conception of the mission of life in a new dimension. At the dawn of a new day, he writes: 'I stand at Your door seeking to know Your will'. The insight that dawned upon him is well expressed in the following lines:

... A way to help others who are in need

That is what today is for me, You tell me

And You showed me the way to life.

With no regrets for the bygone past, and with no slackness that puts off things to an indefinite future, the author got the enlightenment that 'now is the time' that is 'our portion' for investing in fulfilling the mission of life:

> Yesterday has melted away like a night's dream
>
> Tomorrow something I cannot foresee
>
> Only today is the wealth in my hand
>
> A precious diamond the tide of time brings to me.

'The wealth in my hand' is 'today'! Not only the author proclaims this, but at 89, he makes his every 'today' count with further creations – presently working on *'Icons from St. John'* – about 13 woodcuts with matching meditations, which awaits publication.

CONCLUSION

The Song (No. 34) *'The Incarnation of Mercy'* is a prayer for God's mercy adequate for life and eternity:

> Have mercy on me O, loving One!
>
> Have mercy on me since I come to Thee,
>
> Seeking Your mercy!

Being a sinner, the author confesses,

> ... I'm filled with fear,
>
> I lost all peace in my heart.
>
> Seeking Your mercy
>
> I am coming to You,
>
> Have mercy on me, O Lord!

For too long he desired His 'matchless treasure of kindness' but now he comes to Him with this prayer:

> And now I come to You!
>
> Cast out my fear of mortal body;

Draw me to Your safe bosom,

Give me full victory which is with You;

Have mercy on me, O Lord!

The fear of death can be quenched by and only by an unshakable assurance of the eternal life. The longing for 'the whitest robe' which He alone can give is free of all filth and dirt of this mundane world. A supplication is made to fill each realm of his heart and his thoughts always 'with an abiding peace'. A final plea concerns breaking of the rock of his heart 'so that tears of regret freely flow' and wash away his sins. Here is the beautiful imagery of water gushing out from rock as when Moses struck the rock.[14] One of Dr. Raj's woodcuts[15] is titled *'Moses Hits the Rock'*. As Moses smites the rock, there were waters gushing forth to quench the thirst of the day. The author knew from his student days the famous song – *'Rock of ages cleft for me, Let me myself in Thee'*. Here the author symbolically talks of the rock of his heart and the waters are the tears that flow from a broken heart. The author desires nothing but 'a renewed heart' and 'the raiment of righteousness' wherewith he prays:

Holding me by Your hand,

Lord, lead me on!

In the Song (No. 36) **'My Father's House'** the author demonstrates how he could overcome the fears of life and the fear of death, because he has the Lord as his 'light and salvation' and as his 'strong fortress'. And he boldly declares: 'I shall not fear any danger'. And, he further declares:

If all races rise up to kill me

Even if all my enemies rise up to destroy

---

[14] Numbers 20:11.

[15] Published in *'The Bible and the Technologies of the Word'*, ed. by Joseph Palakeel. Bangalore: Asian Trading Corporation, 2007. p. 54.

And an army comes down to fight with me
I shall not be afraid nor shall I fear.

Staying in the Lord's house, hiding in the bosom of the Father, and abiding with Him without fear – this the author considers as 'the endless fortune'. Therefore, he longs to 'abide in the courts of my Lord' forgetting himself, 'Giving thanks to Him' and singing His praises in a thousand tongues.

In conclusion, it is fiting to note that the uniqueness of this 'Bhakti Sahitya from the heart of Dr. P. Solomon Raj' is attested to by a couple of scholars in the theological and literary fields respectively. Bishop P. Victor Premasagar in his Preface to the author's book in Telugu, in addition to his sincere appreciation for all the merits of this *Bhakti Sahitya*, brought out an instance where we find similarities with the writings of Isaac Watson.[16] It is Dr. Job Sudarshan who aptly discerned the striking similarities in these 'Songs of Solomon Raj' with Rabindranath Tagore's 'Gitanjali'[17] for their short passages and deep meaning. With the double advantage of availability of both the Texts in Telugu and English, the present researcher feels this is one of the most comprehensive studies ever made on the 'Songs of Solomon Raj'. However, as mentioned earlier, there are still 11 more songs included in the 'Golden Hits' yet to be reviewed. In recent times, a manuscript with 11 other songs written in English at Sambalikan, the Asian Institute for Liturgy & Music in Manila, during 1990-91 came to light (These are given in the Appendix and a review on these is beyond the scope of the present essay). These seem to be written with some musical notations. Nobody knows how many other songs have flowed from the pen of Solomon Raj, an

---

[16] Compare Song No. 9 with Watson's song in Andhra Christian Hymnal (No.212).

[17] *Abhinandanalu,* in **Gaana Kusumaalu,** Vijayawada: 2002, p. ix.

investigation of which is much in order. It is hoped that this study will not only stimulate interest for further research, but also develop genuine inclination in the use of these songs for personal devotion and ensuing edification. The author's word pictures as his paint pictures are really inspiring to those who read them. It is most fitting to have a few of Dr. Raj's related art works in this book, some of which are world-renowned and with historical significance. The front and back cover pages are also adorned with the author's art works (A list of these art works is provided in the Contents.). The hours spent in reviewing these 'Songs of Solomon Raj', and in overseeing this publication rendering editorial tasks had been personally enriching beyond measure, for which I am grateful to the author.

Dr. B. S. Moses Kumar

IV. Appendices

1) Alternative Renderings

Song 6: The Light in My Soul!

The lamp of love within my soul,
Let it brightly glow, my Lord,
So I show that light to all
And lead them right forward.

For in Thy path of love I go,
And that path to others I show.
Lord of life, You let them see
In my eyes Thy great mercy, the lamp of love.

When darkness comes my face to hide,
Keep me so I'm not afraid,
Teach me now to face the strife,
Help me O, the giver of life, the lamp of love.

When my journey comes to an end
And mine eyes seek the rest to find
In the land where there is no death,
And there will be my second birth, the lamp of love.

Stretch Your arm and gather my soul,
For all my woes at last to heal,
And firmly at Your blessed side
I shall forever and ever abide, the lamp of love.

Song 6: Pray, Put a Flame of Light in My Heart!

Dear Lord, let the flame in my heart brightly glow
So I may give light to all people.

Help me to walk in the paths of Your love
And follow in the footsteps of the Lord of light
So the world may see the light shining in my eyes
Lord, let the little flame in my heart brightly glow.

When the evening of my earthly stay draws near,
Receive me to Your bosom, O Lord,
I come casting behind all fears and all earthly loads
Have mercy on me, Lord, and save.

When the tiresome journey of this life is over,
And I close my eyes in soothing slumber,
Receive me to the deathless land and the nightless day
To the very place where You ever abide.

Song 39: The Brilliant Baby!

As the golden light spread all over the world
Then was He born in the manger, the baby our Lord
And He lighted the universe.
The matchless image of the glorious Creator
And to the sinning humans the great forgiver
Came to bear our sins.

Those who awaited for many generations to see the
Savior
Have today praised God in a thousand tongues for His
favor
And the earth rejoiced.
And to grant the eternal life to humans destined to
death
The source of life today as a little baby came to the earth
As God's great gift.

He Himself to lift us from the curse of sinful grave
Came down with love for us to redeem and save
And He took upon Himself our burdens.

The merciful Lord Jesus in the womb of a virgin
Was born to carry on His shoulders the curse of sin
And came to give us heavenly gifts.

That the people of the earth will cross the ocean of grief
And stand in God's presence finding in Him relief
He foretold His coming to His people
To take us to the world where there is no shedding of
tears
To declare the day of redemption and to wipe away
our tears
He came down to show the Father's mercy.

<hr>

2) Songs from Sambalikan

<hr>

1

The Stormy Skies (96 96 D)

Then sky gets dark and the clouds are razing.
Alas! The way is bleak.
The beast and bird and all creatures
A safe abode they seek.
I tell myself – the Lord is ruling
Whatever it looks like now:
'Tis safe for them who know His keeping
And trust in His great love.

When evening comes and darkness creeps
Mine eyes will close in sleep
To give me healing deep.
I tell myself - the Lord is ruling
What ev'r it looks like now:
It is but those who know His keeping
Can trust in His care and love.

His mighty bosom is my resting place
And there I find peace.
No evil dart can ever reach me
To ever rob me of my rest.

2

The Wondrous Jesus (77)

Wondrous Jesus, Lord and God
Blessed thrice Thy name shall be
Saints and angels do applaud
In the realms we cannot see.

Shining like a brilliant star
Brighter than the sun and moon
Shineth Thy countenance far
Where Thou art 'tis always noon.

Now to my poor inward eye
Sweetest Lord, Thy *darshan* give
While I to Thy bosom fly
Then with Thee I'll ever live.

3

I Heard the Shepherd

Once I heard my Shepherd playing
On His flute the music flowing
Calling me to follow Him.
Then I turned my feet from wandering
Deeply on His great love pondering
In response I heeded Him.

When I saw His hands outstretching
Me and all the world embracing
Offering His salvation great
Then I saw His bosom bleeding
For my sake with God He pleading
Lead me through the Mercy gate.

When I got His sweet anointing
Saving me from fall and fainting
I rested my wounded head.
Then I said He was my keeping
So, for me there is no more weeping
Tenderly He cares for me.

Now always I hear Him singing
Day and night great joy He's bringing
Casting out my fear and pain
All His love for me out pouring
I my life to Him surrendering
Nowhere shall I stray again.

4
The Glowing Hearts

Jesus set our hearts aglow
Let Your light upon us flow
So we may for ever shine
Till we share in glory Thine.

Thou livest in the brightest light
Far beyond the human sight
Nor the angels can unfold
Thy mantle layers manifold.

Thou bestowed Thy grace to me
Dream-like now Thy face to see
And in endless hope to wait
For the day I see You straight.

Then at last when I can fly
Piercing through the clouded sky
Then I see Thee face to face
And feed upon Thy endless grace.

5

I Heard a Voice *(10 5, 10 5)*

I heard the call of
The wondrous lover
Once upon a time.
And then I told Him
I'm His for ever
Blessed be His name.

He never turned His
Face away from me
Mercy is His name.
He always rains His
Showers of blessing
Night and day the same.

We liken Him to
A kindly Shepherd.
Rightly so indeed
He leadeth us in
The greenest pastures
Tenderly to feed.

I made a covenant
To serve Him ever.
May He find me fit.
My life for Him I
Shall freely lay down
It will be profit.

The Holy and Profane (77)

Once the Word had become flesh
To redeem the human race
Then all matter great and less
Was made holy by His grace.

When the Lord had blessed the wine
And the bread He broke and gave,
Was it not a meal divine?
Strong to nourish and strong to save?

Holy, mundane, high and low
So we call things God had made.
But He does not see them so,
None to Him is high or low.

The Evening (77, 77)

When the evening comes at last
And mine eyes shall close in rest
Time and tide away have past
As my soul shall find a nest.
Blessed Savior stretch Your hand
To receive me in Your land.

Loads and cares lay aside
Freely span my wings apart
None can dampen now my stride
As I come to where Thou art.
Gazing up to You always
Till at last I see Your face.

O, my Savior make perfect
All the pathways of my life
Some were crooked some were straight
As I went through the fierce strife
Since it was Your will for me
Spotlessly for Thee to live.

Grant at last that I forget
All the nightmares of this land
And the righteous robe to get
In Thy presence as I stand
Press me to Thy kindly heart
Whence I never shall depart.

8

Who is the Cause? (98, 98, 98)

Who gives my soul great exultation?
Who is the cause of the wondrous bliss?
Who fills my heart with high elation?
Whose is the name that confess
Jesus the Lord and He is my song
Keeping me cheerful as I go along.

Who is the one that died for my sake?
Bearing my sins all to the cross
Watching and caring ever awake
Counting His life for me a loss
Jesus my Lord and He is my song
Keeping me cheerful all the way along.

Who for my sake has crossed the hell?
Who is the source of lasting life?
Who gave to me a story to tell?
Who brings me to the end of the strife?
Jesus the Lord and He is my song
Keeping me cheerful as I go along.

9

The Mother Earth (87, 87, 87)

Mother earth is Your creation,
She will always give her fruit
Feeding us and every nation
All the creatures dumb and mute.
Teach us, Lord! to love the earth
Which to us has given birth.

Sister River, Brother Mountain
Birds and insects big and small
Raining cloud and spring and fountain
You have made for us them all.
May we look them with respect
As from us this You expect.

We have sinned against the Nature
Father do Thou please forgive
Teach us how with every creature
And with earth in friendship live
Keeping safe its purity
Giving for posterity.

10
The Weaver (88, 88)

The weaver goes on weaving still
The universe his loom does fill
I see the garment slowly grow
How it turns out I do not know.

A host of hues come emerging
In various patterns as I stare
But the final shape to emerge
Is yet not known except to Him.

The potter's wheel goes round and round
His fingers on the clay abound
To make a pot as He conceives
And puts it in fire till it glows.

I watch and wait and put my trust
His simple child this do I must
But what's and why's I do not know
Till He alone will kindly show.

11

Forgiveness to Us! *(88, 88)*

Lord, help me now to bear the pain
As I am heard amiss again
Teach me to say a gentle word
To wipe the hurt that I have caused.

Hush up the soul take hurt away
And guard my lips in what I say
So that I may my emotions watch
Before a deadly step I reach.

Slow to judge and slight to anger
Bearing insult slightly longer
Make me pause and help me to know
That final word from Thee should go.

Lord, heal the wounds that I have made
Set right the hearts that I invade,
As now I ask, forgive my soul
May You my rival too console.

A Biographical Note
about the Author

Dr. P. Solomon Raj

Born on February 21, 1921, at Neggipudi, West Godavari Dt., A. P., South India.

Primary & Secondary education - at his native place.

Graduate Studies - B.A. at Andhra Christian College, Guntur (1940-45).

Studies in Education - B.Ed. at Government Training College, Rajahmundry (1947).

Theological Studies - B.D. at Gurukul Lutheran Theological Seminary, Madras (1956).

Ordained Minister of the Andhra Evangelical Lutheran Church (AELC).

Master's Studies – M.S. (Graphics) at Indiana University, Bloomington, U.S.A. (1965).

Doctoral Studies - Ph.D. at Birmingham University, U.K. (1983) Under Prof. Hollenweger.

Doctoral Dissertation – 'A Christian Folk Religion in India'

First published in Germany by Verlag Peter Lang in 1986.

Second Revised Edition 2004 by Center For Contemporary Christianity, Bangalore.

Discarding the traditional mode, Dr. Raj chose an innovative mode in his ministerial vocation! Never confined himself to an appointed parish of limited horizons, but soared like an eagle with renewed strength and vigor - the whole world becoming his parish! His methodology in presenting the timeless message of the Gospel in a timely mode: by means of literary works in Telugu and English, and works produced or reproduced in other languages.

5 Major Works in Telugu (Each A Different Kind of Literary Creation):

   1) *Puja Mandiramu* (Temple of Worship)

   2) *Veda Vinodini* (Scriptural Amusement)

   3) *Eeshodaharanamu* (Illustration of Jesus)

   4) *Kim Kartavyam*   (What Task?)

   5) *Gana Kusumalu* (Musical Flowers)

His *'Liberation in Luke's Gospel'* published in German, Dutch, English, and last of all in Telugu, contains wood block prints with matching meditations on twelve themes of liberation – all taken from Luke's Gospel. Much Published & Most Popular Work: Originally Published in Germany in 1991. Recently Published in USA in 2008 as Meditations for the 12 Days of Christmas.

The unique methodology of Dr. Raj in communicating his message with Christian themes to a global audience had been his three-fold art, namely, Batiks, Woodcuts and Etchings.

➤ **His Works with Batiks:**

1) Living Flame and Springing Fountain *(34 Batiks and Meditations)*

   Delhi: ISPCK, 1993.

   First Published in Germany in German language in 1988.

2) Fiery Wheels: Art Works and Meditations
   Vijayawada: St. Luke's Lalit Kala Ashram, 2003.
   Contains 29 Batiks, 3 Acrylics & 5 Color Woodcuts.

➤ **His Works with Woodcuts :**

1) 'The New Wine-Skins': The Story of the Indigenous Missions in Coastal Andhra Pradesh, India. Delhi: ISPCK/MIIS, 2003.

   Contains 6 Color Woodcuts & Poems.

2) 'Biblia Pauperum : The Poor Man's Bible'
   Bangalore : Asian Trading Corporation, 2008.

   Contains 10 sets of 3 – antitype in the middle, & OT types on either side.

➤ **His Works with Etchings :**

1) 'Etched Icons: Art Faith and Culture' Vijayawada:
   St.Luke's Lalit Kala Ashram, (2009).
   Contains 59 Color & 7 black 'n' white Etchings.

➤ **Research being done on Dr. P. Solomon Raj:**

1) Ms. Marie Dominic Cicilya, *'Dr. Solomon Raj: A Christian Artist'*

Dissertation submitted in 1995 for the Degree of M.A. in History of Fine Arts to the Department of Fine Arts, Stella Maris College (Autonomous), Madras.

2) Jojanneke Dekker of Utrecht University - '*Solomon Raj, Prophetic Artist in India*' (Masters Dissertation).

3) Mr. K. Sam Mathew under the title, '*A Study of Indigenous Symbols in selected 'Batik Paintings' of Pulidindi Solomon Raj as Means of Communicating the Gospel in India*'

   Thesis submitted to the Senate of Serampore College for the degree of M. Th., 2009

4) Dr. B. S. Moses Kumar of Sam Higginbottom Institute of Agriculture, Technology & Sciences (Deemed University), Allahabad – '*Incarnation of the Gospel in the Indian Culture – With Reference to the Art and Poetry of P. Solomon Raj*' (Dissertation being done for Ph.D. in Theology).